MODERN THOUGHT FOR HIGHER EDUCATION REFORMATIONS

MODERN THOUGHT FOR HIGHER EDUCATION REFORMATIONS

The Unification of Faith and Scientism

ADITYA SHASHI JAIN

KALPAZ

Modern Thought for Higher Education Reformations

Rs. 540

ISBN: 978-81-7835-780-5

Published in 2010 in India by
Kalpaz Publications
C-30, Satyawati Nagar,
Delhi-110052
E-mail: kalpaz@hotmail.com
Phone : 9212729499

Lasser Type Setting by: Rudra Computer Graphics, Delhi
Printed at : Gian Ridhi Offset Printers, Delhi

To my mom and dad,
for their eternal care and cooperation

Contents

Foreword

Human beings constantly remain in search of novel and innovative ways for serving people and societies. Nothing else could be better than to think about a better educational and learning system for generations to come. The more developed a society becomes with her educational system and learning institutions, the more becomes the responsibility of her elite citizens for the uplift of the challenged sections of the society. Education can be undoubtedly placed as a foundation on which we can build a world dedicated for personal enlightenment coupled with the participations in altruistic affairs. Author Aditya Shashi Jain's enthusiastic forethought calls for raising such a foundation.

Our nation has been renowned for her grand educational values and ideas with universities like Nalanda and Takshila, which flourished as important seats of learning during ancient times. Today also, our universities are efficiently catering to the varied needs of the society. We have come a long way from the skyscrapers of education based on faith to the budding foundations of modern scientism. The final destinations are yet waiting for us to adopt the modern thought determined for the unison of the two.

We are a nation proud of her tolerance, always promoting peace and harmony even under tough times. Principles of honesty, truth and non-violence are deep rooted somewhere in our civilization. Our sense of unity in diversity, our capability to imbibe ideas from different cultures and traditions, provide a base on which we can count for our modern institutions. In modern times also, nothing much is going to change, the beliefs and the aspirations remain the same. To combine scientism and faith is a cherished dream of our ancestors and should be reflected more intensively in our thoughts and actions. Author's attempt here is looking forward with a sense of completeness and integrity for promoting our social values and also for solving problems of common people. Problems like ignorance, poverty, illiteracy and illusions that we are facing today need to be resolved with strong and sustained personal, social and national commitments. We are in an era when we can search for coordinating methodologies with deeper insight into the social systems. That will strengthen the systems and will provide better ways of understanding problems, and their resolutions. Modernized design of institutions should aim at both developing moral values and problem solving. All this can be achieved only with strong replenishment of our education and new researches leading us to problem solving approaches.

The book aims at sharing an engineering approach that can be developed with the intent of providing platform for different disciplines to join hands, to share their knowledge and finally to come out with feasible solutions. In fact, this approach has been developed especially for a unique nation like ours and it is something that India needs. I hope that the thought of the author with need-based improvements from time to time may prove to be a successful endeavor in the realm of education and learning. At first sight the thought seems to be too abstract to comprehend but the ideas appear to have a potential and creativity. Our sincere attempts can transform our education and institutions serving the cause of common people.

Aditya Shashi Jain is a software engineer and has worked with Tata Consultancy Services for a short period. For the last two years he is engaged in applying his computational analytical skills over social domains and has come up with certain unique ideas for human resource development. I wish him all success in his modest contribution.

I commend this book to the people concerned with higher education, social science and system science researches, the academicians and teachers, political leaders, and especially to the young scholars of the nation.

Bhopal
22 May 2009

Prof. Mularam Joshi
Rtd. Director, Distance Education
and
Professor of English
Barkatullah University

Acknowledgements

I, the author, express my deep gratitude to Prof. Mularam Joshi for giving me his precious time. He extended his guidance for the organization of the book and also wrote an encouraging foreword.

I am grateful to Shri Manoj Jain who was always cooperating me in my endeavor. I am thankful to all my dear friends and akins for their liberal support.

Aditya Shashi Jain

Preface

From the Vedic era to the Modern times, the ideals of learning for man are the same: the search for the eternal happiness for himself and for his society through every pacific means. Education can be considered at the core of the learning process and as such the responsibilities of the education towards any nation are immense. So are the responsibilities of higher education towards the overall education of the nation and hence the nation herself.

The enduring influences of higher education have played a significant role in the social prosperity and scientific, technological and economic development of independent India. Through higher education our governments and institutions have provided great opportunities for the immense human potential to work for bringing a new social order of equality, independence and togetherness in the nation. Our youth is also making us feel proud with their global success stories written within the wondering limited resources. Still, on a greater scale, higher education has not been up to the mark to fulfill the much faster changing needs of the society. Today, it is facing various problems, quantitative as well as qualitative. Reformations in higher education system themselves depend on contemporary socio-political, socio-economic strength of the nation. An awareness of these factors among the citizens would further help in overcoming the challenges that our nation is facing today. For this, the system of higher education needs to be earnest and dynamic enough to understand the significance and the present day problems of the different disciplinary institutions that contribute to the overall development of our nation.

The present volume as a philosophical theme would be an effort for finding reformed possibilities in the field of higher education and learning. Though the thought at present would be quite generic, yet the approach would be very promising for understanding the problems of the domain.

Aditya Shashi Jain

PART - ONE : EDUCATION IN INDIA: PAST AND PRESENT

1

Education Developments The Ages

"Ultimate knowledge is that only, which enables one to release the Absolute. Being acquainted with the Absolute, the soul gets rid of all the worldly sufferings, even the sufferings of taking birth and undergoing death."

-'Mundakopanishad'

Education in Vedic Period

The ancient Indian education was developed by the Vedas and the Upanishads. The literal meaning of 'Vedas' is the knowledge and the word is derived from 'Vid' root meaning 'to know'. Thus 'Veda' means the knowledge of various types.

It is said that the Vedas were not written in the ancient times and they were traditionally inherited by disciples and also sons from their teachers (gurus) and fathers. Thus they were preserved orally. Later on in Mahabharata age they were compiled by 'Krishnadvaipayan' who is also called 'Veda-Vyasa'. He compiled the four 'Samhitas', namely 'Rigveda', 'Yajurveda', 'Samaveda', and 'Atharvaveda':

'Rigveda': The 'Rig-Veda Samhita' is the oldest significant existent Indian text. It is a collection of 1,028 Vedic Sanskrit hymns and 10,600 verses in all, organized into ten books (Sanskrit: *'mandalas'*). The hymns are dedicated to 'Rigvedic' deities.

'Yajurveda': The 'Yajur-Veda' ("Veda of sacrificial formulas") consists of archaic prose mantras and also in part of verses borrowed and adapted from the 'Rig-Veda'. Its purpose was practical, in that each mantra must accompany an action in sacrifice.

'Samaveda': The 'Sama-Veda' (Sanskrit *sâmaveda*) is the "Veda of melodies" or "Knowledge of melodies". The name of this Veda is from the Sanskrit word *sâman* that means a melody applied to metrical hymn or song of praise. It consists of 1549 stanzas, taken entirely (except 78) from the Rig-Veda. Its purpose was liturgical and practical, to serve as a songbook for the "singer" priests who took part in the liturgy. A priest who sings hymns from the Sama-Veda during a ritual is called an *udgâtr*, a word derived from the Sanskrit root *ud-gai* ("to sing" or "to chant").

Atharvaveda: Unlike the other three Vedas, the Atharvana-Veda has less connection with sacrifice. Its first part consists chiefly of spells and incantations, concerned with protection against demons and disaster, spells for the healing of diseases, for long life and for various desires or aims in life. The second part of the text contains speculative and philosophical hymns.

The Upanishads: The Upanishads are largely philosophical works in dialog form. They discuss questions of nature, philosophy and the fate of the soul, and contain some mystic and spiritual interpretations of the Vedas. For long, they have been regarded as their putative end and essence, and are thus known as Vedânta ("the end of the Vedas").

(A) The Vedic Education

According to Vedic worldview, the world is pervaded by divinity and the aim of every living being is to achieve liberation that is possible only through the control of the mind. The agencies of education were the Gurukula, Parishad and the Sammelan. Gurukuls were traditional Hindu residential schools of learning; typically the teacher's house or a monastery. The Parishads were the bigger educational institutions where several teachers used to teach different subject. This may be compared almost to a college of the present times. In the Sammelans or the seminars, the scholars used to gather at one place for discussions and competitions generally on the invitation of a king.

Education was free (and often limited to the higher castes), but students from well-to-do families paid Gurudakshina, a voluntary contribution after the completion of their studies. At the Gurukuls, the Vedic students were taught the four Vedas by heart. Side by side they studied Shiksha, Kalpa, Vyakaran, Jyotish, Chhanfa, Nirukta and logic in general. Only students belonging to Brahmin and Kshatriya communities were taught in these Gurukuls.

The Vedic system of education very much emphasized the importance of discipline in the attainment of knowledge. This, however, was self discipline. The main aim of this teaching was all round development of human life, i.e., the physical, mental and spiritual development of human life.

(B) Brahmanic Education

The post-Vedic period extends between 1400 B.C. and 600 B.C. With the spread of Vedic culture, the sacrificial rituals dominated and the Brahman priests gained the highest position in Indian society. In Vedic education emphasis had been laid on the religious aspects of education, but the Brahmanic education included worldly aspects as well. The aim of education was to achieve self-reliance, self-control, formation of character, individual development, knowledge of social and civil life, and preservation of national culture with the physical development.

Education in Buddha Period

Gautama Buddha was against the rigid classification of the people according to the varnas into the four castes: the Brahmans, the Kshatriyas, the Vaishyas and the Shudras. He established equality among people. He particularly pleaded for simplification of life. It is hence that he ignored metaphysical questions and concentrated upon practical ethics.

Like Vedic education, Buddhist education was mainly religious. Its aim was to attain salvation by living a pure, simple and ideal life. Most of the monks were carrying on the study of teachings of Buddha and Dharma Shastras. In the primary education, reading, writing and arithmetic were taught. In higher education, Religion, Philosophy, Ayurveda, Military training etc. were included. Everyone was free to choose his subjects without any restriction. But in higher education only specialized education was imparted. Brahmanic education was also going on in the Buddhist period. In Buddhist centers also, the subjects of Brahmanic education, such as the four Vedas, History, Puranas, Prosody, Dhvani, Poetry, Vyakaran, Jyotish, Vedanga, Sankhya, Yoga, Music, Ayurveda, Tantra etc. were taught.

Education in Muslim Period

Mohammad Gori laid the foundation of Muslim rule in Northern India. The aim of education during this period was the extension of knowledge and the propagation of Islamic principles, laws and social conventions. Education was based on Religion. Its aim was to make a person religious minded. The Muslim education also aimed at the attainment of material prosperity. The two agencies were 'Maktabs' and 'Madarsas' for primary and higher education respectively. In 'Maktabs' children were made to remember the 'Ayats' of 'Quran.' The stories of Prophets and Muslim 'Fakirs' were also told to the children. Children were imparted the knowledge of art of writing letters and conversation. In Madarsas special emphasis was given to the education of religious as well as secular subjects. The religious education included the study of 'Quran,' Mohammed Saheb and his preaching, Islamic laws and Islamic history, etc. The secular education included the study of Arabic literature, Grammar, History, Philosophy, Mathematics, Geography, Politics, Economics, Greek language, Astrology and Agriculture, etc.

Education under British Rule

British records show that indigenous education was widespread in the 18th century, with a school for every temple, mosque or village in most regions of the country. The subjects taught included Reading, Writing, Arithmetic, Theology, Law, Astronomy, Metaphysics, Ethics, Medical Science and Religion. The schools were attended by students, representatives of all classes of society. The foundation of education was mainly religious.

The current system of education, with its western style and content, was introduced and funded by the British in the 19th century, following recommendations of Macaulay. Criticizing the native literature and language, Lord Macaulay advocated English to be made the medium of instruction in India. He admitted that current Indian languages were almost incomplete, inefficient and lacking scientific vocabulary. Hence, important books could not be translated in those languages. Therefore, Macaulay discarded the local languages and degraded these literatures. The aim of education was to raise intellectual fitness and moral character of the scholars through European knowledge. Macaulay's report led to the closure of the Sanskrit Pathshalas and Arabic Madarsas.

After independence, education became the responsibility of the states. The Central Government's only obligation was to co-ordinate in technical and higher education and specify standards. This continued till 1976, when education became a joint responsibility of the state and the Centre.

Source: This text has been extracted from the book "DEVELOPMENT OF EDUCATIONAL SYSTEM IN INDIA", Vinay Rakheja - C/o R. Lall Book Depot, Meerut, by Suresh Bhatnagar, Anamika Saxena, and Sanjay Kumar. UNIT- I Part-1, 2, 3 and UNIT-II Part-4.

2

Higher Education in India Present Needs

"Refrain from illusions, insist on work and not on words. Patiently search the divine and scientific truth."

-Mendeleev's Mom's dying words to Mendeleev

Since independence a number of committees came into existence from time to time to study the issues and challenges regarding higher education and providing roadmap for future expansion and excellence. A great deal of good result came up. But the rapid growth in population and the increasingly need of the colleges and universities always eclipsed the positive aspects of our educational growth. Today, the rapidly growing industries and organizations are marching towards new milestones of economic success in their fields and are waiting for the realm of higher education to match on to their pace. But not all is fine with the system of higher education in our country. Some general issues of concerns that continue to prevail in our system are like irrelevant curriculums, lack of practical approach, non-professional orientation, low standard of teaching quality, limping research facilities, improper infrastructure, imperfect examination system etc.

It is mainly the system of higher education, which sooner or later takes care of the entire system of education. Modern education in India is often criticized for being based on rote learning. Emphasis is laid on passing examinations with high percentage. Very few institutes give importance to developing personality and creativity among students. Recently, the country has seen a rise in instances of student suicides due to low marks and failures, especially in metropolitan cities, though such cases are very rare. The boards are recently trying to improve quality of education by increasing percentage of practical and project marks. A great deal has been done. A great deal is going on. And a great deal needs to be done.

To begin with, we may have a quick look over the present broader needs of higher education. What the leaders have to say about the higher education, and what the related figures justify:

Big Words on Higher Education

(A) Dr. Manmohan Singh
Prime Minister, India.
Mumbai, 22 June 2007.

Addressing the faculty and students of the University of Mumbai on the occasion of the institution's 150th anniversary, Dr. Manmohan Singh said: -

- A quantum leap in approach to higher education is needed if India was to capitalize on its "latent" human potential.

- "Almost two-thirds of our universities and 90 percent of our colleges are rated as below average on quality parameters. And most importantly, there is a nagging fear that university curricula are not synchronized with employment needs."

- "Our university system is, in many parts, in a state of disrepair. We need better facilities, more and better teachers, a flexible approach to curriculum development."

- "We need to also upgrade the quality of the higher educational institutions so that they work on the frontiers of knowledge, harnessing its immense capabilities for our common societal benefit." he added.

- "While we do have much to be proud of, we also have a long distance to travel in the field of higher education and research in India to attain world standards. We are at an important cusp in our developmental trajectory. We are at a point when the dynamics of our population growth can catapult us into a prolonged cycle of rapid economic growth - growth which can be the basis for eradication of the ancient scourges, poverty, illiteracy, ignorance and disease," Dr. Singh said.

(B) Shri Arjun Singh
The Then Human Resource Development Minister, India. New Delhi, 11 October 2007.

Inaugurating the two-day National Conference of Vice-Chancellors on Development of Higher Education, Shri Arjun Singh said: -

- The time has come that the academic world of the country to reform higher education to make it come to terms with reality.

- Higher education today is the 'sick child' of education, and is not serving the cause of young people of India.

- Our country needs a road map for higher education.

- 'Experimentation' should be the key word while carrying out reforms in higher education.

- The parameters of higher education as to what should be the content, what should be the extent of higher education, what should be the methodology of teaching and what should be the basic ingredients of the syllabus etc. needs to be defined.

Member of Planning Commission Prof. Balchandra Mungekar in a similar concern said "Between 1857 and 1986, we have presided over a failed education system. The general education system has been divorced from the Indian reality. It is now time to redraft the entire curricula".

"Today, not more than 9-10% graduates are employable. There is a totally diverse economic and social reality. The task is to drastically restructure the education system," Prof. Mungekar added.

(C) Professor Yash Pal
Eminent Scientist, Former Chairman of University Grants Commission (UGC).
02 Jan. 2008.

- Asserted that creativity is possible only when one steps out of his/her discipline.

- Why must we be imprisoned in narrowly defined disciplines? Nothing in the universe, even in daily life around us can be contained within a single discipline. Why the walls around disciplines so impervious? When it does, most creativity oozes out of these walls. We need porous boundaries.

University Grants Commission (UGC) has decided to prepare a curriculum that will incorporate inter-disciplinary courses to make it compatible with the modern-day requirements.

- We will try to introduce everything which is related to life. This will mark the beginning of a knowledge revolution in the country. Education is for enhancing the knowledge base of students. It relates to the day-to-day affairs in life.

- Education is about how to handle the situation confronting the common man. It could be Globalization or any other common problem", he added.

(D) National Knowledge Commission (NKC): Note on higher education, 29th November 2006.

- Higher education has made a significant contribution to economic development, social progress and political democracy in independent India.

- It is a source of dynamism for the economy. It has created social opportunities for people. It has provided a beginning for the creation of a knowledge society. But it would be a mistake to focus on its strengths alone. It has weaknesses that are a cause for serious concern.

- It is clear that the system of higher education in India faces serious challenges. And it needs a systematic overhaul, so that we can educate much larger numbers without diluting academic standards.

- We recognize that a meaningful reform of the higher education system, with a long-term perspective is both complex and difficult. Yet, it is imperative.

- First, it is essential to reform existing public universities and undergraduate colleges. Second, it is necessary to overhaul the entire regulatory structure governing higher education. There is an urgent need to restructure the system of undergraduate colleges affiliated to universities.

- There is a clear need to establish an Independent Regulatory Authority for Higher Education (IRAHE). Such a regulatory authority is both necessary and desirable.

National Knowledge Commission has raised a number of issues and challenges related to higher education and has recommended a number of reforms both general and special for higher education in its - Note on higher education, 29th November 2006. The ideas are under processing.

Some Statistics on Higher Education

- The proportion of our population, in the age group 18-24 that enters the world of higher education is around 7 per cent, which is only one-half the average for Asia.

- India has about 350 universities. It needs a massive expansion of opportunities for higher education, to 1500 universities nationwide, that would enable India to attain a gross enrolment ratio of at least 15 per cent by 2015.

- The present support for higher education, at 0.7 per cent of GDP, is simply not adequate. In an ideal world, government support for higher education should be at least 1.5 per cent, if not 2 per cent of GDP, from a total of 6 per cent of GDP for education.

Source: National Knowledge Commission: Note on higher education, 29th November 2006.

'Life in the coming decades is likely to bring new tensions together with unprecedented opportunities. To enable people to benefit in the new environment will require new design of human resource development. The coming generation should have the ability to internalize new ideas constantly and creatively. They have to be imbued with a strong commitment to human values and to social justice. All this implies better education.' [DES04]

The forethought of National Policy on Education 1986 continues to ring true. In a country facing the challenges of poverty, illiteracy, unemployability etc., all good opportunities for higher education needs to be converted into all good achievement. Changes would be indispensable and changes should be continuously searched for. A lot of efforts has been going on but certainly would need to be catalyzed to meet the much faster changing needs of the society. For this catalytically support, I think, a complex, heavy-weight and pragmatic philosophy would be a most suitable art to build which will help in connecting the old precious thoughts with the modern latent ones, yielding a proper design for describing the problems and the requirements. Before that few abstract ideas for abstract considerations are:

- General problems, first, for understanding and solutions would need general awareness and speculations about general ideas.
- Higher education reforms focus should be less on the replication of quality and should be more on getting rid of the obsoleteness.
- Higher education focus should be more on requirements rather than on generalization or specialization.
- How more quality can be generated with investing minimum of additional time, money, other resources and efforts?

What all and the only thing anyone would need in the 21st century and after, would be a dependable and replicable methodology for generation of understanding of various disciplines and better coordination among them. As the learning reformations would be a long-term and continuous process, hence it's important that the existence should be respected with all the ventricles and all the auricles and should be comprehended with all the neurons and all the dendrites so that the scholars can learn rightly this way. It is not hard to know 'what' needs to be done, but 'how' things happen over a period of time, only the history and the makers of history can tell.

3

Macaulay and Indian Education

The Ism of Change

"Education is the thing we have done worst in India, I believe, because we have provided education for the mind only and not the character. As a result the average educated Indian has little character and no discipline. They will have to learn both if they are ever to be a nation."

-Lord Wavell
In his farewell letter to the King

Recommendations of Macaulay almost ended up here or it can be concluded that they never began in a true sense. Thomas Babington Macaulay (25 October 1800 – 28 December 1859) was a nineteenth-century English poet, historian and Whig politician and Member of Parliament for Edinburgh. A very influential figure, he came to India in the year 1834 and convinced the Governor-General to adopt English as the medium of instruction in higher education, from the sixth year of schooling onwards. Many people related to education often remember him as the founder of English education in India. A lot is there to learn from his wisdom and a bit is there to forget about his exaggerated involvements. Let the education pay tribute to the young man, a progressive scientific thinker, who with all good intentions had no other option other than to shatter the then present philosophies of education for solving problems of that time.

Macaulay in India

The Languished History: In 1834, there was a controversy in British India over the language to be used for Indian higher education. On the one side, there were the British Orientalists who wanted to use Sanskrit, Persian and Arabic and on the other side there were the Anglicists who had scorn for Oriental languages and Indian culture and wanted to enforce English. Macaulay landed in India with a lot of premeditation, at the height of this debate and soon published his famous Minute, which sealed the case for the Anglicists.

Later India gained independence on the grounds that Macaulay was thinking would come to end with the advancement of English education. Since then wishes had been there also to get our education freed from the ism of Macaulay. However, he was not just on his government duty. He was in the duty of the laws as well. He certainly helped us, but since then his legacy has also raged many with his malicious comments over a great culture admired very rightly at the very wrong time by many of his emotional colleagues. However, Macaulay's decisions towards any civilization were more based on its alive outward facts rather than her buried inward history. Before the man, who somehow failed to learn many things about all of the Gods, but just managed to learn nothing else but the one word 'justice' for his world, it was a simple case of a typical civilization with her masters having knowledge of the 'Three Worlds' and the 'Absolute' and the Master's relatives and followers in the dominance of the smattering of one of the most intelligent animal on a planet lying somewhere in the corner of one of the billions of billions of galaxies of their universe. And it's not like that the lawyers are bad at heart but sometimes they need to take decisions with a broken heart. And its not like that lawyers don't have faith on the Laws of God but they always keep in mind that at times human beings would be helpless in the hands of homo sapiens. Interesting.

The Enticing Future: For a nation like ours, the best reform could be a perfect coordination of the scientific thinking and religious philosophy. In Swami Vivekanand's view, for the development of a balanced nation, we have to combine the dynamism and scientific attitude of the West with the spirituality of our country. The entire educational program should be so planned that it equips the youth to contribute to the material progress of the country as well as to maintaining the supreme worth of India's spiritual heritage.

However, today philosophy is far from implementation. The mere figures are much heavier on the philosophy of ages. In any situation, the few simple steps would be: appreciating 'the good' there is, acknowledging people due to whom 'the good' is there, candidly accepting the weaknesses and finding better solutions with more of dedication and more of rationality. What ultimately is more important for education is not just the rough ideas of the intellectuals but their conversion into the plane principles in the minds of people.

On the real grounds, understanding the diverse needs and the problems of a society that is rich in diversity of cultures and nature of works, in terms of thoughts, would be necessary for change but will not be sufficient for more than a billion people. The modern thought would like to depend a lot on first understanding the problems in evolutionary terms to present situations and then moving on to concepts, to analysis and designing things and would have no option other than to define first the problems from end to end. First the reality in terms of the philosophy: what all is there and what all would need consideration: from forethought and emotions to money and flow diagrams. But before that, time for the civilized lawyer with his bitter doses of arguments. After all only arguments would come to rescue.

Lord Macaulay

and

Indian Higher Education Reforms

Getting rid of the ism of Macaulay for the formal education won't be a difficult task. It would be certainly impossible. For this, what anyone would have to do is to just stand on his shoulders and look farther from him and for the rest, higher education would need reformations...

Macaulay

Why reforms are needed? Are there any problems with the fundamentals? No. Not at all. And there would be never. Still a change would be phenomenal. So what all options are there? This question should now begin in the young dynamic minds of the nation. After emerging from the education system, a young mind, for the values and significance of education, should acknowledge Macaulay, his allies and the people who have worked for betterment of education, and for its drawbacks, if any, the best choice would be soul-searching leading to self-discipline or else, simply education system should be reformed.

What could be worth reform? Reformation is more about rethinking. It is more about esteeming and learning from the worth is there. So, a reform would be rethinking about the eternal basics, esteeming the basics of different disciplinary institutions and learning for a better coordination among them. What would be needed won't be simply higher education reformations, but a rethinking that would lead to a renaissance, commencing from anytime and ending up with higher education reformations. This would simply be an understanding of the worth knowledge that always lies in the history. Let the education begin with thinking of the history of Macaulay's age: his awareness as well as his seeming ignorance - both worth to know.

Macaulay and the worth knowings: Macaulay's major role was somewhat away from the core of education but he still remains a part of educationist's celebrations and cerebrations. In his minute on Indian education he said- "The whole question seems to me to be, which language is the best worth knowing? I have no knowledge of either Sanskrit or Arabic. But I have done what I could to form a correct estimate of their value. I have read translations of the most celebrated Arabic and Sanskrit works. I have conversed both here and at home with men distinguished by their proficiency in the Eastern tongues. I am quite ready to take the Oriental learning at the valuation of the Orientalists themselves. I have never found one among them who could deny that a single shelf of a good European library was worth the whole native literature of India and Arabia. The intrinsic superiority of the Western literature is, indeed, fully admitted by those members of the Committee who support the Oriental plan of education".

All Orientalist's swans were geese. All Macaulay's mules were horse. For the well being of the Sanskritmen and the Arabicmen, the differently cultured thirty-five years young Englishman rather Earthman went unaware of the immenseness and solemnity of Indian literature due to his obvious disinterests and the non-availability of the things and beings he was looking for exactly. However, had he met the ambience of the freedom movement it certainly would have forced him to conclude that something indefinable yet special is there behind the Indian literature that needs attention of the whole world. Still the story wouldn't have finished there. This smart Lawman would have never thought of leaving the art of his mother discipline behind and just performing clergy activities for influencing the civilizations to come. Rather than being sentimental and anticipating the people to just become all time followers of eternal principles of idealism based on time-being and poetic rationality, he would have taken parallel decisions more based on the deep-rooted academic fundamentals, science of mental life and the present realities. So here was the failure for the second time to learn a bit from the ism of Macaulay. Though learning wouldn't have brought any success. For Macaulay, languages were fine symbolic tools for digging the mines and treasures of knowledge and the most amazing thing about the barrister was that he knew which tool comes to help when, as he continues in his minute:

'...At the close of the fifteenth and the beginning of the sixteenth century almost every thing that was worth reading was contained in the writings of the ancient Greeks and Romans. Had our ancestors acted as the Committee of Public Instruction has hitherto acted; had they neglected the language of Cicero and Tacitus; had they confined their attention to the old dialects of our own island; had they printed nothing and taught nothing at the universities but Chronicles in Anglo-Saxon, and Romances in Norman-French, would England have been what she now is?...

And it's not like that this Lawyer was just a master of transferring knowledge in shortest, fastest and most efficient possible manner but he was an equal expert in the case of monetary matters as well, as he continued in his "Government of India" - A speech delivered in the House of Commons on 10th of July 1833.

"......In a pecuniary point of view, therefore, I conceive that we can defend the measure as it affects the territory. But to the territory the pecuniary question is of secondary importance. If we have made a good pecuniary bargain for India, but a bad political bargain, if we have saved three or four millions to the finances of that country, and given to it, at the same time, pernicious institutions, we shall indeed have been practising a most ruinous parsimony. If, on the other hand, it shall be found that we have added fifty or a hundred thousand pounds a-year to the expenditure of an empire which yields a revenue of twenty millions, but that we have at the same time secured to that empire, as far as in us lies, the blessings of good government, we shall have no reason to be ashamed of our profusion......" So never be shy of talking about money.

Also the smart lawman was aware when to follow laws and when to get them follow the human beings, also when to be courageous and when not to be shy of being a timid as he continued in the same speech -

'......This, then, is the state in which we are. We have to frame a good government for a country into which, by universal acknowledgment, we cannot introduce those institutions which all our habits, which all the reasonings of European philosophers, which all the history of our own part of the world would lead us to consider as the one great security for good government. We have to engraft on despotism those blessings which are the natural fruits of liberty. In these circumstances, Sir, it behoves us to be cautious, even to the verge of timidity. The light of political science and of history are withdrawn: we are walking in darkness: we do not distinctly see whither we are going. It is the wisdom of a man, so situated, to feel his way, and not to plant his foot till he is well assured that the ground before him is firm......'

The firm grounds of the reality: Macaulay, to give more credibility to his decision, noted that students at the Calcutta Madrassa were being given stipends for studying Arabic while they willingly paid for studying English. He also mentioned a petition by ex-students of the Sanskrit college who mentioned that they were jobless after giving up a good part of their life in learning something that did not get them food and that there was no demand for Arabic and Sanskrit books that the committee had printed at great cost. So, English was the right justification on the basis of facts available to him. Because even today, at the end of the day, things would end up in justifying things against the major reality that is the lack of money. English would be needed as soon as possible, for making more money. At the same time, 'Sanskriti' would be needed as soon as possible for giving direction to that money and the moneymakers. And need not to worry about Sanskrit, may be in a century or two it will rule this world, but that would be due to the equal efforts of the Englishmen.

Macaulay's Legacy: Though mundanely an alien, still, he did his level best for us. He was certainly a prospicient man with a tough thinking dedicated for providing lasting solutions for the Indian outlooks of that time. He did not think that it was British duty to educate the lower classes directly. His goal was to teach the educated class, create what he called "enlightened natives" and get them to diffuse the knowledge to their countrymen and here was a failure for the first time to learn a bit from the ism of Macaulay, though learning wouldn't have brought any success - "I feel that it is impossible for us, with our limited means, to attempt to educate the body of the people. We must at present do our best to form a class who may be interpreters between us and the millions whom we govern; a class of persons, Indian in blood and colour, but English in taste, in opinions, in morals, and in intellect. To that class we may leave it to refine the vernacular dialects of the country, to enrich those dialects with terms of science borrowed from the Western nomenclature, and to render them by degrees fit vehicles for conveying knowledge to the great mass of the population"- he almost concluded in his minutes and here would be an opportunity to learn a lot from the ism of Macaulay as well, though learning won't bring any success.

So, getting rid of the ism and especially the arguments of Macaulay won't be a difficult task for the formal education. It would be certainly impossible. An intellectual like him and that too a barrister could never be replaced. For this, what anyone would have to do is to just stand on his shoulders and look farther from him as a major role of education would be the same fight against the same acts of pseudo-religionism, which still claims for the superiority of spiritualism over mundanity (are expected to wait till 2135). Also that would be the most justified place to begin with. At the same time more people would be needed to defend our own great culture of wisdom, which is likely to show the civilizations the way to peace and the ultimate literature. All these people would be needed after 2135, but planning should be started from now.

Now let the higher education make Macaulay's reliable skills as a true and talented barrister, his typical self-defined duty of taking his Lord in too much of confidence, his hyperbolic art of making his emotional opponents to enjoy their time and their salary at home, all this unconscious and think again and ahead for the generations to come. And it's not like that anyone would fall in love with lawyers but no one would have any other option. Remember *'bhaye bin preet na hoyi'*. So if u have faith in Religion then beware of God's softwares and if you have faith in Democracy then beware of Lawyers.

The Thinking Learners: The sensible learners are the soul of our education system. True education is a way of empowering them with the knowledge gained from within and outside, which assimilates within their mind and soul, helps them in understanding the ideals, the environment, the mutual differences, and always inspires them to work with strong determination and perseverance to minimize these differences for bringing happiness for them, their world and the future worlds.

Now a major objective of higher education is to prepare the learners for handling the differences. Still, the differences should be manageable on a scale of optimality for them and it is always the responsibility of the experience to work together and make things go easier for the coming generations.

The Inspiring Teachers: True examination of a teacher does not lie in teaching the learners but in inspiring them to learn and learning from them. Our teachers are the backbone of our education system. They play a major role in shaping the mental sphere of the learners that finally leads to the social happiness and prosperity of the nation. It is the profession that leaves most important and lasting influence on the society. Especially in a nation like ours, developing with the principles of democracy, where people proudly enjoy a great deal of freedom and the success of systems, in an ideal and dignified manner become highly dependent on the mutual understandings efforts of the citizens themselves, the role of teachers become very prominent. It should begin with enlightening the minds of the pupils with curiosity and should end with leaving them as autonomous learners. They would also need more in-depth thinking now and if possible salary as well and with more of the defined responsibilities.

And The Big Generation: True examination of an education system would not lie in supplying of the ideals but in withstanding with the unfavorable reality. A lot depends on the big generations. Famous American Jurist Oliver Wendell Holmes, Jr. has said that a child's education should begin at least one hundred years before he or she is born. Education is a precious thought and a beautiful dream shared by the older generations with the younger ones. The success of education for learners depends largely on the panorama provided to them by their elder generations. A learner is more likely to follow rules because the people especially the elders around are doing so. And it is good to learn this way rather than doing things just because of the fear factor. After traveling through rationalism, good habits should be followed finally with an unconscious state of mind.

Present Scenario: Today, situation at the implementation level is very complex but quite natural and interesting. Politicians have rightly declared our higher education as a 'sick child' of education. Many educationists and knowledge intellects with their sweet dreams often broken by the impervious government membranes are rightly seeking for an independent regulation for higher education. But primarily, true examination of education system won't lie in getting rid of the impressions of else-disciplines but in the promotion of self-discipline. Dreams need to be converted into strong designs before ideas can proceed for the implementation details. First, finding better alternatives in the core of education itself would mainly help in getting out of any situation in a sustainable manner. What is not needed is a rethinking that would depend on Politics. What is needed is a rethinking of which Politics would be an indispensable and a very important part. People are working hard in every dimension. Still, problems are there. Though they are not exactly human-made and have come to us in an evolutionary manner, still would always wait for further initiations for the long-term solutions. For more it would be all about the approach after 2025.

The approach for the knowledge and feasibility in thinking: Whether it is the realms of Science and technology, that of ancient Religions and philosophies or others, human beings have touched almost a state of idealism in every sphere influencing mankind. So what's left now? Now, true examination of education system won't lie in replicating its quality but in getting rid of its obsoleteness. Success of education system would now mainly depend on the approach towards the oceans of knowledge. For the fulfillment of objectives of overall education system, higher education system would need to get more relevant focus. Finance was supposed to be the only constraint but the concepts are also proving as constraints. For maintaining the interest and concerns, reformed concepts would be indispensable. Majority needs to move from philosophical abstractions towards real time executions, towards application and result oriented thinking and activities. A requirement engineering approach may help here in converging things. This approach would deal with something that lies between the ideality and the reality and that is the feasibility. Learning from the clever problems would also help a lot in finding solutions. A saint can be a good saint, a politician can be a good politician, an educationist can be a good educationist but problems they are master of all with their heads and tails in every dimension. For their treatment on time, the different disciplines would need to come together. Together a system-oriented thinking would be needed. This would help in capitalizing disciplinary originality and setting back the faith of the majority in their own systems. All this should begin from the young minds of the nation after 2025.

Research Oriented Rethinking Frame Work: For enough flexibility to experiment with and design a curriculum-framework with further dedication towards life-like, professional and vocational-orientations a much stronger research and development framework would be all-important. Programs for identification of gifted talents and natural inclinations should become a part of normal plan as far as feasible and as soon as feasible. True examination of education system would not lie in handling the rules but in handling the exceptions that often make the rules for the rules. This primarily would begin as a matter of learning and understanding, the significance and the scope of a curious and a thinking mind. It's always really inspiring to have Maulana Azad National Institute of Technology, Mahatma Gandhi Medical College and Jawaharlal Nehru University. But a curiosity remains there: why something like Isaac Newton Institute of Science and Technology or G. J. Mendel Medical College or Bertrand Russell University etc. are not there? Acknowledgements should go global now and not just in the thinking but in the expressions and in the executions as well. And that's the only way - planning after 2025 should be there to lead the world.

The Ultimate choice: Education is about reaching people. Higher education is about reaching the young mind. The extent of higher education is God's brain. Higher education reformations would never simply be a set of activities that would need performance or simply planning that would need administration but really it would be a dream that would need everyone. We are far more than a billion people with a rich and poor divide. It would be no less than a struggle, a struggle for not just existence, but a struggle for existence with excellence. It would be a revolutionary process that would enhance the evolutionary thinking and would take few decades of patience and hard work. May be several.

Finally, true examination of education system would not lie in searching for the better solutions, but in encouraging people's potentials for solving problems. Let the education be not Englishmen's choice. Let the education be not Sanskritmen'sor Arabicmen's choice. Let the education be simply people's choice. After all education system does not need people, but people need education system.

So many people have worked hard and are working hard towards education. Lot of good and promising research work is far from implementation due to various reasons viz pseudo-political interventions, financial and human resource constraints. Let the education once again try to find some more pearls of thoughts and ideas from the same oceans of knowledge in an ultimate engineering fashion.

PART - TWO : HUMAN ENGINEERING: THE THOUGHT

4

Human Engineering

"I do not mean that those who want to search after truth through external nature are wrong, nor that those who want to search after truth internal nature are higher. These two are the modes of procedure. Both of them must live; both of them must be studied; and in the end we shall find that they meet."

- Swami Vivekananda

Introduction

Any thing less then this would never work for education and is something that is known since ages and is what education is looking for. Till the two natures would meet, metaphysical questioning would help in keeping them together. Is it like that only how this world is? What, if given a chance by the almighty, would be an achievement for we humans to create: a gorgeous heaven for the good, a terrible hell for the bad or a pacific earth for the commons? The aim of education in the upcoming 'Human Engineering Age' would be simple: leaving behind a far more beautiful earth for the generations to come.

The Last Query: To say "Modern thought for higher education reformations" would not be enough to comprehend what exactly needs to be conveyed, where the thought would fit-in and what are the rationales behind it. Let's get back from the philosophical text stream and move on to work asking few straightforward questions for having a brief about the focus of the thought. Also a system would never become comprehensible in a systematic manner. It would take time. Just stay with it for long.

What is the aim of this set of questions?

To signify the focus on higher education through the human engineering approach.

What exactly would be the human engineering approach?

An approach for understanding problems on a larger scale.

Why the term 'human engineering'?

Engineering refers to the discipline dealing with the art or Science of applying scientific knowledge to practical problems. Education should be about character building with solving problems.

What sort of problems?

Major social problems like unemployment, illiteracy, and lack of awareness and problems of higher education.

What are the measures for solving problems?

There are different disciplines and systems for solving problems like: political system, economic system, administrative system, laws and legislature, education and various other disciplines. So all these disciplines and system approaches are measures for solving problems. Present focus is on higher education. It would help further in economic as well as human resource development.

What are the expectations from higher education? How are they likely to be fulfilled?

Education needs to deal with the feasibility for bringing reality near to ideality. Reality can be supposed of various disciplines, systems, statistics and personal-view. A new approach could be multidisciplinary higher education model with a system approach of thinking.

Why this multidisciplinary approach?

The world is like that. If I say world is a set of disciplines and world is a system, the latter sounds more precise. At age around 17-18 young minds are most developing and become progressively conscious about the real world. They are supposed to be more socio-holistic in knowledge, understanding and thinking before becoming dedicated for a single discipline. Also, it would be good to know a little about roles and responsibilities of people of other disciplines and the problems that they are facing. All this would be for few, and for understanding the problems of higher education.

Why system oriented thinking is important for few students?

So that they can decide what rest should do. Interesting. For knowing and understanding how concepts travel through complexities as they are taken towards implementations. It would deal with something that lies between ideality and reality and that would be the factors of feasibility. Also an understanding of how systems come into existence, how complex and well established they remain, would be useful. In addition, in systems study there would be no place for cramming. It would not be much about reading books, but about applying thinking and analytical power. It would enhance observing, reasoning and writing skills, creativity, knowledge generating capabilities, application, result-oriented and real-time thinking. It would help in turning ideas into design and further implementation as a systematic process.

What is this system?

With this approach in general, a system would be defined as an entity with well-defined boundaries, set of rules and regulations, organizational structures, procedures, roles, responsibilities and authorities of the people, together converging to fulfill a set of common objectives. A system can be as big as our education system. It may be a comparatively smaller system like a library management system.

The following is the summary of the thought: This commencing chapter gives a glimpse of the concept. To understand the significance of higher education, the best way would be to have a systems-view of the world with a human touch. To handle the complexities that would be faced while reformation of such a comprehensive system an engineering approach would be the best. The chapter says that education is a system dedicated to the process of learning and the overall development of the students depends on the elderly environment. Simple.

The next chapter would be a concise recall to the importance of education, the objectives of the learners, the roles of the teachers and the knowledge factor. It would then describe a reformed knowledge base education model for the higher education development.

The third one would brief about an interdisciplinary engineering approach that would provide the platform (from concepts and planning to implementation and maintenance) for the overall reformation of highly complex systems like that of higher education and the systems that influence the overall learning process of the students.

The penultimate chapter would be a collection of some of my thoughts and ideas that I hope would provide the readers an interesting recall into the fundamental of the disciplines, present needs and problems of the society and the rationales behind the comprehensive human engineering approach.

The last chapter details how the thought can be taken towards implementation along with some issues regarding the present approach of learning. Here financial and administrative aspects related to higher education would not be taken under consideration as the thought itself would take about two decades of research, planning and development. The concept may talk about some general changes in the system so for more precisely describing the picture for implementation aspects an institutional approach would be considered as more efficient option.

4.1 Human Engineering: A Blossoming Philosophy

Human engineering is a learning philosophy for bringing solutions for human beings in an engineered manner. It would be a way of understanding humans with the intent of making things easier for them and their environment by solving their problems and providing consultancies to them. To begin with, would need a fundamental knowledge and understanding of various disciplines and an interdisciplinary approach. It would then ask for an extensive awareness of diverse needs and interests of human civilizations: from basics to material to scientific needs, from entertainment to emotions to spiritualism, the ways they get fulfilled, an understanding of their environment, their effect on their environment, the effect of environment on them and the systems surrounding them. It would move ahead with refining knowledge and understandings:

from abstract philosophies to simple necessities and from simple necessities to complex systems. Together, it would progress with the study for understanding and engineering systems. It would analyze the changing necessities, and would search for the reformation feasibilities of the systems for their fulfillment. The dynamic necessities would be made comprehensible, both in an analytical and holistic fashion by following an engineering school of thought.

4.2 The Scheme of Things:

4.2.1 Systems Engineering: The Mother Philosophy

Systems engineering is an interdisciplinary field of engineering that focuses on the development and organization of complex artificial systems. It integrates other disciplines and specialty groups into a team effort, forming a structured evolutionary process that proceeds from concept to development to performance and administration.

The Focus: For software-based systems, the process of systems engineering comes before the process of software engineering. Instead of concentrating solely on software, systems engineering focuses on a variety of elements, analyzing, designing, and organizing those elements into a system that can be a product, a service or a technology for the transformation of information or control [RSP01].

The Understanding: Before problems can be solved, the system in which they reside must be understood. To accomplish this, the overall objectives of the system must be determined. The role and responsibilities of the people, the procedures, the structure of the system, controlling systems and other system elements must be identified and functional needs must be elicited, analyzed and modeled [RSP01]. The importance of systems engineering process lies in the fact that it provides a platform to start the process of solving the problem by initiating the process of understanding and to have a hold on the problems from the very higher levels of abstraction.

The Requirements: At the end, an overall system requirement specification is prepared by the process of requirement engineering. This process provides the appropriate mechanism for understanding what the system wants, analyzing need, assessing feasibility, negotiating a reasonable solution, specifying the solution unambiguously, validating the specification, and managing the requirements as they are transformed into an operational system [RSP01].

The Evolution: In ancient times there was a discipline: the Religion. Not just in books but in the air as well. There used to be a king as the sole administrator of his reign. Kids used to go together to the 'Gurukul' for their education away from their home. Saints and Saints like used to be the teachers. Their disciples used to study different disciplines embraced by the mother Religion. Time changed, rules changed. With the advancement of British rule things went out of the control of the old mother Religion. Different disciplines grew more complex, independent, dominant and accountable. India got independence after a long struggle with the British. It was people's rule. Administrators were people's choice. The Religion of the nation became her Laws and her Constitution. So everything was still fine. But rules being made by men were expected to be changed by men for their own comfort. Being a latecomer to the scientific and industrial development our nation faced challenges in every age. The major system changes were unfeasible but were needed for fulfilling the dynamic needs of the society. As a rule of thumb a system like that of education needs to be 'unthreaded' in every twenty five to thirty years of time to find possibilities for major changes and if that fails it is likely to be complex and problematic to do changes in it with progressing time. Again, time is changing, rules are changing.

At times, in the morning it used to be 'slate-batti' and 'pag-dandees' now it used to be big bags and heavy wait in the vehicles, in the night it used to be the stories of the 'raja-rani' with 'dada-dadi' now it is something different with televisions. Changes need to be accepted happily. Change is the law of nature. And change should be the law of human beings.

Coming to higher education, reformation in higher education would be near to an impossible job. A system so complex, well established and dependable would always be a hard nut to crack. It would need to be understood to each of its ligaments and tendons. In any case, our philosophy should remain ready to accept everything from complexities to chaos to legacy damages. A possible approach to curriculum development would be to have a curriculum with a developmental approach. The traits of system engineering philosophy with a human touch would be very close to the day-to-day activity of humans. It starts its journey from the basic requirements, provides a better insight into the problems, platform for thinking over them, preparing documentations and finding alternatives solutions and sharing them. It gradually incorporate the people, the knowledge of various other disciplines, rules and regulation, constraint, factors of feasibilities as they are needed for the details of the fulfillment of the needs. It would be the best way for connecting ideas into design. Also, when problems are complex that too in a complex system, it would be good to make the unconsciousness of a system conscious on paper. For this, this approach would prove to be a better choice.

But here would be a major complexity from concept to development to performance and administration. If any new possibility there, from concept to development it would be a different set of human beings, from development to performance it would be a different set of human beings, from performance to administration it would be a different set of human beings.

So all the way it would be human beings and not systems. Interesting.

4.2.2 The Human Factor: Systems do not Need Humans, Humans Need Systems

Though influenced and analogous to the system requirement engineering philosophy, but it will not be exactly a system requirement engineering approach. This approach would focus more on the needs of human beings and would starts with them. Say, system requirement engineering philosophy for systems of social domains. Systems approach has been employed since last few decades for understanding and solving complex social problems. However our philosophy first, would like to depend upon the simplicity of human beings then after it would search for the complexities of systems approach of work. Humans here will not be considered as part of the systems, but systems would be the basic needs of the humans. Humans will not be considered only for their roles, responsibilities and authority within the system, but their participation with a well-defined role-profile in the system would be a part of their life. Simply saying, humans first as beings then as resources. It would care for them. It would expect from them. Finally, would state that every social system for its success would mainly depend on humans and well coordination among them, and changes.

Why Engineering? We humans, from learners to the leaders, need to perform many distinct activities in a number ways in our daily affairs. We remain surrounded by number of complex and highly dynamic problems with widespread domain of influence. Doing things in a number of manners and together helping in solving problems in a systematic manner over a long period becomes a tedious job. So the school of thought that would be researched for finding out the possibilities for diluting the problems with maximum resource and effort would be 'engineering'. 'Engineering' would help further in moving: from philosophical abstractions towards system answerabilities and to real time executions, towards application and result oriented thinking and activities. The term 'engineering' may seem odd with human beings, but originally its no machine related. It is related to the term 'engine' that derives from the Latin *ingenium*, meaning "innate quality, especially mental power". I hope its importance would get clear with the upcoming topic of knowledge engineering as a part of education system and the briefing on social systems engineering.

4.2.3 Ignited Minds: Shaping the Budding Learners

Human beings are affected by environment and they affect their environment. Now a bit of thinking about the importance of environment as a set of systems in which the education system is considered as a formal system dedicated to the learners for understanding their world, gaining knowledge about it and finally to have an optimistic effect on their environment. The rest of environment very clearly has a profound effect on the learners, but in a less formal and more casual manner. So, as far as learning would be considered the environment would also play a major role in shaping the ignited minds.

4.2.4 The Environment: A System of Systems

Famous American Jurist Oliver Wendell Holmes, Jr. has said that a child's education should begin at least one hundred years before he or she is born. The success of education for learners depends largely on the ambience provided to them by their elderly generations. A child is more likely to follow traffic rules because the people especially the elders around are doing so. After traveling through rationalism, good habits should be followed finally with an unconscious state of mind.

For this, the study of education and learning would follow a holistic way of thinking: all the properties of a given system cannot be determined or explained by the sum of its component parts alone. Instead, the system as a whole determines in an important way that the parts behave. Such thoughtful of images of environment would need to be there in the minds of people all the way from leaders to the learners.

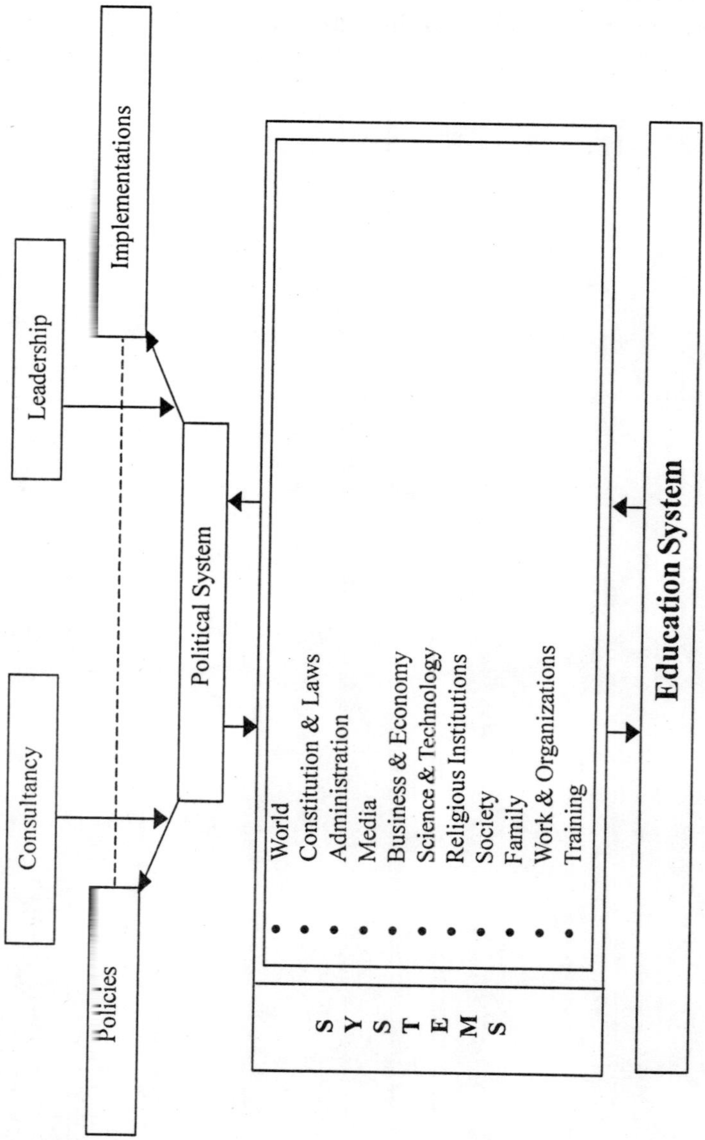

Fig. 1. Education and Environment

5

Education System

"Education is an endless journey through knowledge and enlightenment."

-Dr. APJ Abdul Kalam

5.1 Education: The Soul Necessity

Swami Vivekananda a great Indian thinker realizes that the tremendous emphasis on the scientific and mechanical ways of life is fast reducing man to the status of a machine. Moral and religious values are being undermined. The fundamental principles of civilization are being ignored. Conflicts of ideals, manners and habits are pervading the atmosphere. Disregard for everything old is the fashion of the day. Vivekananda seeks the solutions of all these social and global evils through education. With this end in view, he feels the dire need of awakening man to his spiritual self wherein, he thinks, lies the very purpose of education.

Education simply is to bring happiness from within and outside, for this moment and forever. In any age whether ancient, medieval or modern, men remain in search of happiness both by external nature and internal nature. We Indians would always love our education to be driven by the internal forces but the external dependencies would always be a challenge for us. The thinking is changing and accepting the reality now. We would have to rely equally on both.

5.2 Education: The Philosophy

At times, education simply used to be knowing the ideals and following them. Now definitions are changing and getting complex. Education now should be also about character building by knowing the ideals and following them and by knowing the problems and solving them. Now true education is a way of empowering learners with the knowledge gained from within and outside, which assimilates within their mind and soul, helps them in understanding the ideals, the environment and the mutual differences, and always inspires them to work with strong determination and perseverance to minimize these differences for bringing happiness for them, their world and the future worlds.

Like many great thinkers, prophets and philosophers, Gandhiji was convinced that injustice, violence and oppression manifest from human heart and that education can play an effective role in developing a wholesome human personality capable of resisting war, violence, injustice and oppression and building a social order wherein man can live in peace and harmony with others. Since education is a potential instrument of man making and social engineering, he concentrated on an education that could draw out the best in the child—body, mind and spirit—for developing a peace loving human personality. Gandhian philosophy is, indeed, rich in its educational and social values. It can transform the destiny of man and is capable of establishing an alternative social order if it is practiced sincerely and honestly in its true perspective.

5.3 The Learners: The Focus of Education System

The future of any nation lies on the shoulders of her young generations. The world needs to understand them and they need to understand their world. The education is supposed to take care of them and later they would be supposed to take care of education. The following points would need to be considered as guidelines for understanding the broader necessities of education system:

- Personal development of the learners as good citizens of the nation.
- Cultivation of self-learning capabilities and habits.
- The career objectives of the scholars.
- Domain specific scholars who would take human knowledge further.
- Scholars who later on would play crucial roles in the socio-economic development of the nation and the world.

The responsibilities of higher education are immense. It should bring the learning potential and the natural resources together to raise our standard of living, it should produce leaders with intellectual analysis and imaginative insight so as to promote a new social order based on democracy, justice, liberty, equality and fraternity (University Education Commission). [DES04]

5.4 The Teachers: The Backbone of Education System

Teachers play a major role in shaping the mental sphere of the learners that finally leads to the social happiness and prosperity of the nation. It is the profession that leaves most important and lasting influence on the society. Especially in a nation like India, developing with the principles of democracy, where people proudly enjoy a great deal of freedom and the success of systems, in an ideal and dignified manner, become highly dependent on the mutual understandings efforts of the citizens themselves, the role of teachers become very prominent. It should begin with enlightening the minds of the pupils with curiosity and should end with leaving them as autonomous learner.

But today, it is near to a slip disc. Teachers are getting meager salary and attention as well. There is a wide gulf between the teachers and the students and three major factors, I believe, are irrelevant courses, natural and cultural changes. In the realm of the human engineering approach being a teacher would first mean a person making his or her livelihood through this means. Before teachers would take further responsibility of caring the society, society would have to find feasibilities of taking care of their teachers. Though economy would remain a major constraint but a better sky blue print for future should be there.

5.5 Present Education System: The Qualified Knowledge

The one and only limitation considered about the existing higher education system is that, today, the knowledge bestowed to the learners in it is necessary but not sufficient for accomplishment of objectives of education. Many degree courses are just fulfilling the formality of making students just eligible for other matters or simply to be labeled as educated. Degrees need to be brought out from the narrow focus. For majority it would have to move from theoretical aspects to making them a disciple of pragmatism and master for taming problems. And it's not like that if our education system would not follow that route people won't become practical. They would naturally compensate for the weaknesses of education systems but certainly they would never respect the system of education that is there. They would deny that their education has brought sufficient meaning to their life and their society, something that was expected from it. At the same time never underestimate the greatest significance of present system that lies in its theoretical aspect that would be the foundation of any education system. Simple question - who will take the knowledge further? If simple options would be there for all, who would like to handle the tough, old, boring theories? A big problem. But answers would have to be brought on earth.

5.6 The Knowledge Factor: The Decisive Necessity

What so ever are the problems, what all is dependable for finding solutions is just knowledge. Knowledge brings power, power brings decision, decision brings happiness, and happiness brings independence. Whether it was the Vedic age or the present the purpose of knowledge would be the same forever, only etymological distinctions of the words would be there. Knowledge could be thought of from different views like:

- **Spiritual view:** Its soul purpose is to serve mankind and humanity independent of any Religion, race, nation and region, in a humble and generous manner, and finally leading to enlightenment.

- **Normal view:** It is the appropriate collection of information, such that its intent is to be useful. It is the data and information in the human mind that along with the process of thinking is supposed to enrich understanding and finally leading to wisdom.

- **Systems view:** Knowledge plays a vital role in the success of the decision making process both at personal and organizational level where accountability is crucial. A good comprehensive knowledge base is therefore an indispensable part of the decision support system.

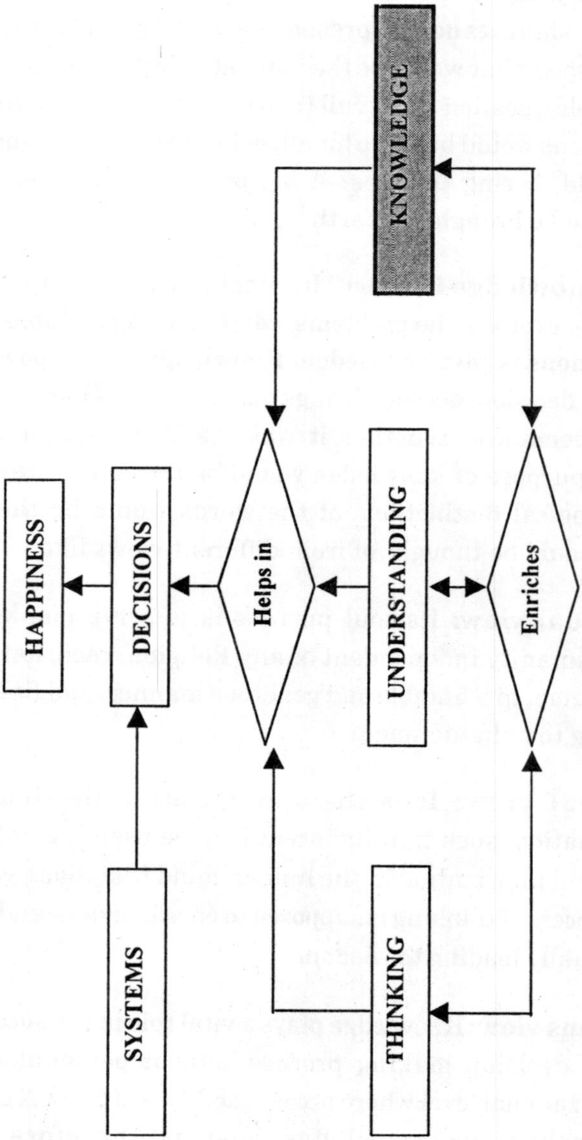

Fig. 2. The Knowledge Factor

When it would come to knowing about a system as complex as our education system, as diverse as our nation, and as dynamic as our problems, managing knowledge would be an interesting task. It would be good to take help of engineering philosophy to break the 'knowledges' and then to recreate them according to our needs.

5.7 Engineering Knowledge: Preparing the Knowledge Base

Knowledge Engineering refers to the building, maintaining, and development of knowledge-based systems. Various activities of knowledge engineering specific for the development of a knowledge-based learning system for students would be as follows:

- Assessment of the necessities.
- Identification of the required knowledge domains for fulfillment of the necessities.
- Presentation of knowledge.
- Development of a knowledge-based system shell/ structure.
- Integration and maintenance of the knowledge structure within the existing system.

The following are the two broad fundamental necessities:

- Curriculums comprehensive enough to maintain the importance of the fundamental concepts and the real time applications and
- Together dedicated research oriented curriculums for science, commerce and arts needs to be maintained.

The following way would be to proceed for the knowledge domains:

Some thinking needs from learner's perspective are realizing their world, development of thoughts skills supporting in the decision-making process or say solving problems. Now keeping two things in mind that complex problems are quite interdisciplinary in nature and things can mainly depend on knowledge at different levels of abstraction and systems for finding the solutions, the knowledge of different kinds would be distributed in following two classes:

5.7.1 The Knowledge of Disciplines:

Discipline means to instruct a person to follow a particular code of conduct, or to adhere to a certain "order", or to adopt a particular pattern of behavior. In academic terms, it refers to a body of knowledge that is being given to - or has been received by - a disciple. It can be further classified into following two broad categories:

5.7.1.1 The Knowledge of Laws and Principles:

This comprises of the knowledge of laws and principles of various macroscopic disciplines viz Religion, Science, Mathematics, Literature, Laws, Political Science, Management, Economics etc. The presentation should follow an evolutionary approach as knowledge is gained through ages in terms of its origin, reasons, importance, progress, merits and demerits.

The lessons of Religion and Literature help in:

- Personal development as a good being.
- Realizing social and personal value of life.
- Developing moral and ethical way of thinking and working.

- Understanding our society, cultures, traditions and heritage of knowledge.

Science support in:

- Developing curiosity and observing skills.
- Enhancing reasoning and analytical abilities.
- Promoting logical thinking.
- Mental development.

Concepts of Political Science assist in:

- Understanding the significance of systems based on authorities and responsibilities.
- Realizing the factor of answerability attached with any system.
- Distinguishing the importance and sensibility of public systems.

The Fundamentals of Laws support in:

- Knowing the rights and responsibilities as a citizen.
- Understanding meaning and importance of justice in complex situations.
- Developing ability to think from others perceptions and an unbiased thinking.

The knowledge of Economics and Management facilitate in:

- Providing feasibility to ideas at policymaking.

- Understanding developing and maintenance needs of systems.
- Realizing importance for proper and efficient use of resources.

To say more about the importance of these disciplines would not be the good use of resources. In fact covering of the contents with the maintenance of their comprehensibility within limited time and space would be a major challenge. Every discipline would have its own issues and challenges. The primary aim would be to develop an understanding about the fundamental concepts of the disciplines and the logics behind them.

5.7.1.2 The Knowledge of Capabilities and Maturities:

This class of knowledge comprises of the knowledge of achievements, potentials, strengths, capabilities maturities and weaknesses in various disciplines. The statistical knowledge of resources, necessities, their trend over a period of time and their comparison on the globe with others nations helps us in knowing where we stand as compared to others.

5.7.2 The Knowledge of Systems:

The intent of knowledge lies in solving problems and for that we can mainly depend on systems. Socially, a system can be defined as an entity with well-defined boundaries, set of rules and regulation, organizational structures, procedures, roles, responsibilities and authorities of the people, together converging to fulfill a set of common objectives. The knowledge of laws and principles, capabilities and maturities comes into action mainly through systems. The knowledge regarding systems is further classified into following two categories:

5.7.2.1 The Knowledge of Existing Systems:

This part comprise of the knowledge of the existing systems, their structures, elements, and importance and how they have taken shape, the system governing systems, the current policies and procedures of the systems. It would deals with 'what systems' there are and 'what systems' have been adopted. A lot of knowledge remains about the systems (The list of systems in heading 1.2.4 - The Environment) due to day-to-day activities, learning and experience.

5.7.2.2 The Knowledge of Engineering Systems:

This category of knowledge would comprise of approach for understanding and reforming systems and designing new systems. For the student, the systems initially would be comparatively smaller ones with lesser complexity. The contents would be a theme of few pages. It would need application on a system (say a library management system) for generation of a document regarding the system's objectives, overall operations, resource requirements and maintenance. The aim would be to introduce students with the fundamentals of systems and the best way would be allowing them to design systems.

This separation is just a broader classification and a more conscious representation of the world-view of knowledge that we come across in day-to-day activities. So this knowledge base is something can be used for the reformation and maintenance of our education system. How? Next chapter would discuss things in detail.

5.8 The Knowledge Base Education Model: The Integration Prospects and Heuristic Thinking

The Knowledge base education model (KBEM) would depict the worldview of higher education. The model will prior need a considerable amount of maturity of neural networks for its implementation. For this, the systems requirement engineering approach can be used for large-scale study of problems and necessities of higher education. There would be a number of options and there could be immediate setbacks. Lot

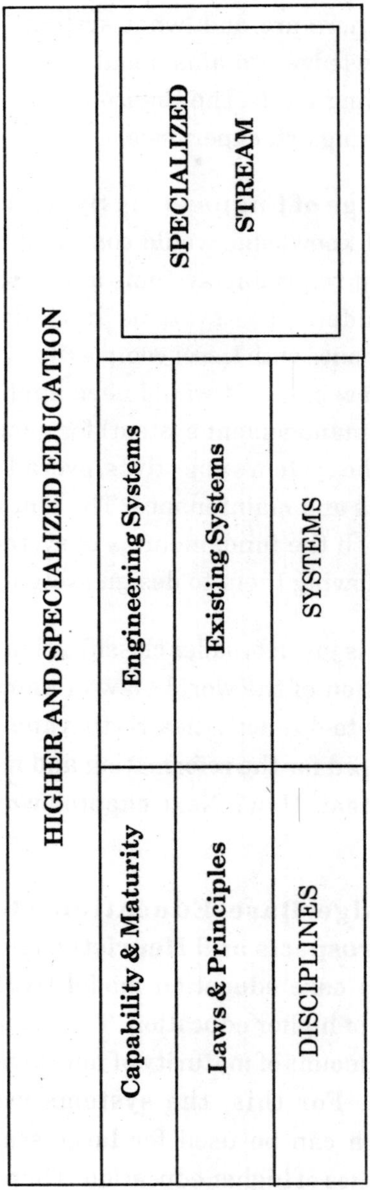

Fig. 3. The Knowledge Base Education Model

of questions would need answer like - what degree courses to be reformed? What about the existing resources? How the good ideas would be connected together with the threads of feasibility? The large-scale approach would be discussed in the next chapter. And the best approach would be generalizing the complete system in two terms: problems and requirements and that is just stay longer with the system.

Now getting back to theory and thinking of the model independent of anything.

The model could be thought of from four different heuristic approaches. These are:

- **Behavior of knowledge:** The evolution of knowledge with blending of disciplines with one another from applications perspectives and then need for the management of knowledge with systems approach as the number of disciplines increased in numbers.

- **Domain of knowledge:** The model would deal in the world-view of knowledge first then may enter into the interest-view or professional-view of knowledge.

- **Distribution of knowledge:** The fundamental concepts remain distributed with different disciplines in different brains. Human engineering approach would attempt for more centralization of knowledge and would help in bridging the intellectual and understanding gap.

- **Levels of knowledge:** Concepts flows from generic levels to specialized levels in a single discipline. This approach would collect generic knowledge of different disciplines then may move forward in the existing manner into specialized domain.

Let's have another general viewpoint: human societies follow certain rules and regulations. When these rules and regulations are enforced through an authority this gives rise to the philosophy of laws. Again for handling violation of rules and regulation penalizations are enforced through laws. When the rules and regulations are accepted voluntarily and their violation does not lead to any penalization process then this gives rise to something like the philosophy of Religion. Now on large scale it needs the supervision: whether rules and regulation of the authority are being followed or not and for this a set of people get engaged in something that gives rise to philosophy of Politics. This philosophy of Politics serves many other purposes like changing the rules and regulation for the welfare of society, providing and managing various services to people on a larger scale. Now this setup needs money, its production and proper distribution thus gives rise to something like that of the philosophy of taxation and Economics. The philosophy of management is equivalent to that of Politics in terms of the supervision of the rules and regulations at execution and the real time and handling exceptions but it is devoid of the authority for changing the higher-level rules and regulations.

Every discipline has some unique feature inherent to human thinking and actions:

Religion	:	Faith and Sacrifice.
Laws	:	Justice and Fear Factor.
Politics	:	Responsibilities and Power.
Literature	:	The Life and The Common Man.
Economics	:	Who has declared Economics as a discipline? May the soul rest in peace.
Management	:	Real Time And All Time Complexities.

The one and only, and the final stoppage of knowledge express after disciplines would be systems.

The possible advantages and disadvantages of this model would be:

5.8.1 Advantages of KBEM:

- A highly dynamic and convergent approach.
- Gives weightage to the various macroscopic disciplines.
- Develops an analytical and holistic way of thinking.
- Develops solution oriented thinking with an interdisciplinary approach.
- Gives a widespread all round pictures of the problems.
- Cascading effects of decision-making become more visible.
- Catalyze the process of understanding.
- Potential for solving problems resulting out of the non-evolutionary division of mental labor.

5.8.2 Disadvantages of KBEM:

- The model, as far as I can think, is absolutely free from any kind of disadvantage.

5.9 Moving Ahead: Realism Against Idealism

There may remain comprehensive differences between the ideals of principles and approach, as found by the learners in the books and the working systems as a part of the real world, in which they work later on or are influenced by. These differences crop up in a cumulative manner because of number of static and dynamic factors that can be broadly thought as:

- Lack of proper education and profession-oriented learning and training.
- Personal values, importance attached with work.
- Personal behavior, human psychology.

- Inherited working habits, culture, traditions and environment.
- Problems of legacy damages, the platform to initiate with.
- Competitions, financial factors.
- Insurgencies, priorities, dependencies, lack of resources, deadlines.
- Various constraints, controls and regulations.
- System structures, system deadlocks,
- Internal system malfunctioning, external system malfunctioning.

And many more. These differences give rise to a number of problems that start making space for future and new problems for future.

5.10 Moving Ahead the Other Way: From Realism to Idealism

A major objective of education is to prepare the learners for handling these differences and to work together, with applying best of their efforts, for minimizing these differences. Still, the differences should be manageable on a scale of optimality for the workers. On a regular basis education would have its own limits of dealing with the reality. Yeh one possible alternative that can emerge from education is changing the reality. It is not like that only higher education needs a systematic overhaul. Together, the idea for greasing the environment too won't be a bad one. For this the working systems influencing the young minds could also be analyzed from various aspects as frequently as feasible for modifications possibilities so as to get rid of the problems cropping up. Systems requirement engineering philosophy would serve the purpose for understanding the problems and developing feasible solutions and hence may help the systems to move from realities towards idealism.

Now as higher education is a means to many ends, so for the system of higher education first step would not be getting into it but getting out of it and roaming a bit into its long lasting significance upon society. First all this would need an approach more external and more unbiased: different nation, different history, different culture, different phases of scientific, economic and democratic development and different quantity and different characteristics of human resource requirement.

Before moving ahead an interesting idea to ponder. This idea was propounded by Prof. Yash Pal in a lecture at M G University Kottayam, on 26 November 2003 as part of University Grants Commission (UGC)'s Golden Jubilee Lecture Series. It went like this:

"......There are many tricky areas where social sciences and physical sciences need to work together. This is required even for defining what would be a good society and furthermore the means to achieve it. Lot of new thinking is required in economic, political and social spheres. If done without including scientists and engineers even the new would be copies of what obtains elsewhere or impossible to achieve. For all this to happen we need to break walls and couple. Couple and engage out with society. I am sure that if we design our education and research enterprises this way all the other problems would resolve themselves......."

'Many tricky areas', 'social sciences', 'physical sciences', 'good society', 'work together', 'new thinking, defining, achieving', 'economic, political and social spheres', 'scientists and engineers', 'break walls and couple', 'couple and engage', 'design of education and research enterprises', 'resolution of all the other problems' - anything left within these 106 words, Yeh, great opportunities for *'chaosphiles'* (chaos lovers). Our UGC is really working hard. Seems that *'bude bharat mein fir se nayi jawani aane wali hai.'* Before that more of chaos is about to come and a possible way to get out of it.

6

Social Systems Engineering

"Don't try to control the players, just change the rules of the game"

-Complex Systems. A rule of thumb

6.1 The System Enlightenment: Independence from Human Dependence

The orientation of players should follow the orientation of the procedures as mentioned abstractly in the normally entertaining rule of thumb. This to perfection will include designing systems as less dependent on humans as possible and supplying intelligence and power inherited through the complex procedures. A more ordered education system would be a first achievement towards human independence or say system enlightenment. Now who will help the system enlightens? Let us begin and learn something from master machines and their masters as a tribute to the mother logic.

6.2 Software Engineering: Learning for Helping Machines

The learning approach for social systems engineering would be quite comparable with the ways the software engineering scholars understands and learns concepts for designing software that runs on machines for solving human problems. However, I think, it would be crucial to mention here that the concept never went developing along this route. Also, analogies should not last longer. Still, the comparison is an easier mechanism to grasp the human resource necessities for the overall social system development process.

For designing computers based system and application software the scholars learn the fundamental concepts of various subjects related to computer science like computer architectures, data structures, operating systems, database management systems, networking, algorithm design and analysis, programming concepts and programming languages etc. These concepts together provide a knowledge base that helps the scholars or the developers in the decision support system during the process of systems engineering, software development, deployment and maintenance.

For overall project development, they understand various software development life cycles models, an engineering and managerial approach and various modeling languages for representations of the problems during different phases of development cycle. Basically, software engineering is all about transference of quality understanding of system requirements from humans to machines.

6.3 From Machines to Humans: The Learning Opportunity

Man and machines are helping each other since ages. Man made machines, machines made machines; now machines are helping man in understanding man and nature more closely, and making far better machines. So, in my opinion, there would remain an opportunity to learn a lot from machines: the way they solve problems for humans and bring comfort along with challenges. Again computational analysis of social systems is in air now. Different people are using it for different purpose.

6.4 Social Systems Engineering: Learning a Great Deal for Helping Humans

When it would come to reformation of a complex system like that of higher education, concerned with human race, the engineers would need to have good understanding of a model say a 'human engineering model'.

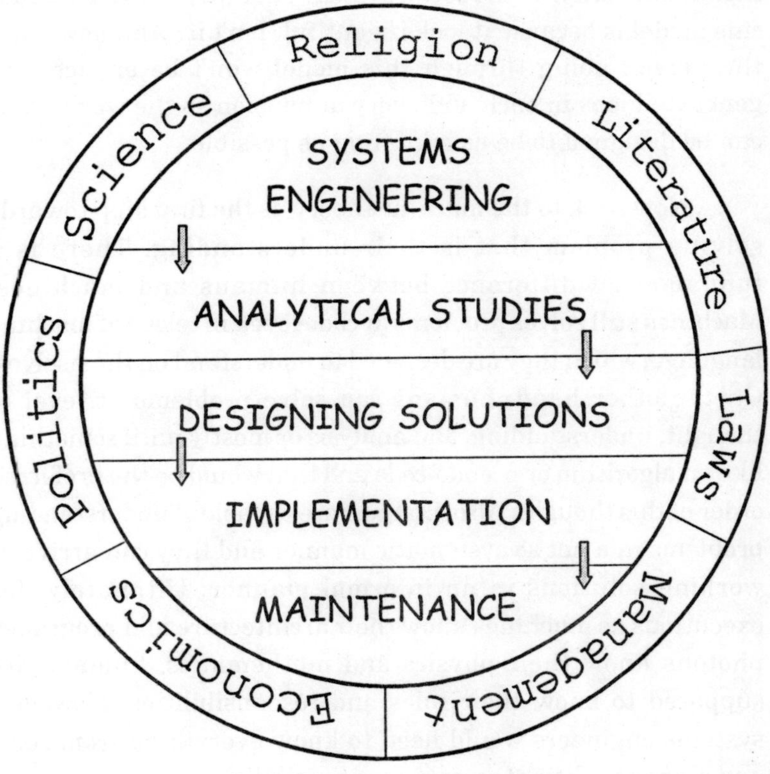

Fig 4: Human Engineering Model: The Logical Awareness

This model in the worst case would cover the fundamental concepts of subjects or disciplines like Religion, Science,

Literature, Economics, Laws, Politics and Management as a part of system logics. Again this awareness oriented understanding together would provide the knowledge base that will assist the developers in the decision support system during the process of higher education system developments. For understanding and reforming existing systems and designing new systems, the revived approach of systems engineering as explained in brief in the upcoming sections would prove to be more beneficial. Here concentration would be on the system of higher education as the social system. And why I am sure about this model is because it looks beautiful. Isn't it? And now since the person going through this model won't be expected to generate ideas in each and every dimension so the world-view can be designed to be as minimum as possible.

Now back to the machine theory as the first step towards solving problem that is their understanding. There is a fundamental difference between humans and machines. Machines still solves problems at code level, in terms of machine language, which they are designed to understand on themselves. On the other hand, humans can solve problems at level of thought, understanding, and analysis or mostly until something like an algorithm or pseudo-code and that would be the preferred order of this thought. Also, humans are capable of understanding problems in a not so systematic manner and they can arrive at working solutions in an informal manner. Ultimately, for executions as machines know their architecture and programs; photons know their physics and mathematics, humans are supposed to know their roles and responsibilities. However, systems engineers would need to know everything from roles and responsibilities to worst-case possibilities.

The model again could be thought of from the four heuristic approaches as discussed earlier in section 2.8-Knowledge base education model. Here more emphasis would be on systems engineering and analytical and holistic studies. Also systems approach would be the least unsystematic approach for understanding problems. The approach would be quite satisfactory irrespective of success or failure and would be almost a final one.

6.5 Thinking About Disciplines: Drops from Oceans

Let us recall some of the major disciplines. Same ancient, gigantic disciplines, the much older, the much stronger is the need of their logic. Few drops of same thoughts from the same oceans of knowledge and the most important thing about human engineering is that it would not believe in making anyone a master of the disciplines but simply a disciple of the masters and above all applicable.

6.5.1 Religion:

Religion should always be given an elderly respect as compared to other disciplines because it is the only discipline generously dedicated for the transformation of homo sapiens into human beings. I believe, those who transform with the help of Jesus and Bible are called Christians, those from Rahim and Quran as Muslims, those from Ram and Geeta as Hindus and so on. Moreover, it is good for human race that no single Religion has monopoly over it.

Religion is the most professional discipline because of the similar nature of the universe and the laws governing the universe. Lord Mahavir summarized this behavior in his statement 'Live and let others live'. Yet it holds no legitimate accountability, and is normally based on faith and beliefs. This set of faith and beliefs can be defined at three different levels of understanding namely: philosophy, expression and execution. Philosophically, it is something for which humans are created. It is meant for quality of thoughts and promotion of moral and ethical way of thinking and living. Different Religions share almost same core philosophy but differ mainly at the level of expression. These expression are the generally the acknowledgements extended by the followers towards their religious heritage and their caretakers and gives rise to the customs, cultures and traditions. Execution is the understanding of saints and disciples about their Religion that provides totality to its true definition and the ultimate value in terms of their thinking, behavior and actions. It is the most visible part of Religion.

Religion could have got the credit of being mother of all the disciplines but it failed from time and time in the hands of pseudo Religionists. Problems injected by humans into the Religion could be solved by humans only and in a humanitarian manner. In the minds of the people, it should get rid of its rigidness and irrationalism by democratic, meritocratic and scientific means, so as to bring Religion back up to its ancient glory. Promotion of religious preaching should go in most rational manner by avoiding window-learning habits and traditions. What mentioned in books would remain quite static, but circumstances are very dynamic and intelligently felt by few. What good saints are saying, a revived discipline needs to be drawn out of it. And of course should remain ready to take help of other disciplines. There is a lot that could be learnt from the fundamental and original concepts of her refined babies of political science and laws in terms of responsibilities and justice. Remember, if Religion is the proud and conscious mother of the 'disciplines' its unfortunately and unconsciously the grandmother of escapism and premature satisfactions.

As far as her re-entry in education is concerned would need to have patience and plans. What all anyone would need for the philosophy and development would be a divine's advocate of the order of Gandhi and for the implementations and maintenance that would be a devil's advocate of the order of Macaulay.

6.5.2 Science:

Hire some people for life long. Give them everything they want. Ask them to read and learn everything available about this universe in both specialized and generic forms as far as feasible. Examine regularly their status. After some sixty years tell them that now you have become someone like God and now tell how you would have created this universe and how it can be preserved.

As much knowledge as many conclusions, after then possibilities and searching the things the other way: from a possibility to where things have reached so far. And it's not like that truth is known, but what is known has an impression on the world or not. So, at anytime or in future things should be applicable and that is what Science is all about.

Science is most innocent of all the disciplines, it never claims for knowing the truth still with all its good intents it would bring some problems for the future generations. Today its global warming, tomorrow, it might be something like DNA warming. The world is already running some thirty-five years late as far as DNAs are concerned. Listening to scientist properly at proper time may dilute the problems as it is becoming difficult to get near to the truth with the help of Mathematics as a language for understanding nature. For more dilution, giving a worldwide central control over certain business of science to more of scientificness would never become possible in the absence of aliens. Anyway, 'super-power' nations should plan more intensively for becoming more 'super-emotional', more 'super-sentimental', more 'super-scientific', more 'super-ethical', more 'super-democratic' and more 'super-planner'. All this, I think, won't need more 'super-intelligence' but consideration over more 'super-stupid' and more 'super-absurd' ideas first. Rest should be left for the responsibilities and the authorities of 'the most of the civilized' and 'the least of the barbarous' aliens.

6.5.3 Political Science:

ϕ#^ω∀∋$Δϑε□ℵ⊗%+∂ς|*(^. Whoops. Sorry some corrupt data in the keyboard cable and problem with the backspace key. For the only few of the most endangered of the mammalians, the stars in the gloomy sky, the lighthouse in the giant oceans, the oasis in the desert, the blood in the body, the needle in the compass, the grammar in the sentences, the chlorophyll in the green leaves, the pi-mesons in the nucleus and the phosphate-bonds in the DNA, known as the good politicians, politics and governance are the most systematic, authorized and widespread way of serving the society. For all this there is no limitation regarding the order of sacrifice, the order of intelligence and the order of patience that they are supposed to have. They could work for 24 hrs a day and that too continuously for some mere 80 years and at the same time they won't be paid for any of their job at the right time and at the same time they would have to answer about each and every activity that they would be performing. Anything less than this won't work. Look how intelligent our western ancestors were in designing things and how simple they have made good governance. Only our good politicians failed to learn from them.

Good governing bodies are most intelligent, except they commit one mistake in their life. As happenings go easier for the people, they become difficult for the leaders and when they are difficult for people they becomes easier for the leaders. Politics, at large, I think, never received the importance and understanding that it deserved. At the end, as such, I think that either Politics might finish in next twenty-five years or the system will become a fossil remain of democracy and no one would be responsible for that situation. And its not like that there would be dearth of good and honest people but there would be more and more and more and more.

Still any premature effort for mitigating the importance of political system should be reconsidered. Politicians should think of themselves as the evolutionary and the curious Kings and should continue to work like a social servant. They should continue thinking of human beings less than eighteen years of age that includes generations to come and should try to impress people above eighteen. For this simple task few of the evolutionary and the curious kings would have to think at three levels of abstractions (time (for day dreaming, wool-gathering and star gazing), money (for food, shelter and clothes), a bit of concept (for reverse engineering, and mental and physical division of labor) and continuity of all this would be their headache) and all the king's men at two levels with supplied poetic documentation over long term of period.

If was feasible, we could had thought of human independence by inheriting better controls through systems procedures and giving more stakes to the people by a more distributed form of democracy: a set of the representatives would have the right to go and ask a set of people and right to implement after twenty years may be thirty. This could have satisfied all type of ideologies and might have brought politicians job at comparative ease. As far as corruption is concerned, whether that related with the moral and ethical values or with the disorderness in the systems, its remedies would always lie in the ignited minds of the school going kids. It will go the way it has come from. In this *'ghor kalyuga'* God is more impressed by the men of decision making than the men of principles. But he keeps an eye: whether the decisions are moving right in the direction of principles or not. Interesting. And as far as education of politicians is concerned it is a matter of debate. At present politics can plan for having an ounce of knowledge of education and tonnes of faith on education.

6.5.4 Laws:

The so declared corroded laws handles most sensible of the human cases: from death sentences to the cases of mercy killings. It also suffers from the suffering provided by human beings. It works under all situations and would never leave anyone in enigma. The lawyer hired for the case proved to be a deceiver by going illegally against his favor. Now hire two lawyers, one for the original case and another for the previous lawyer. And this could be done infinite times because laws both as a necessity and as a responsible authority and without any hurry would provide a way under all circumstances and anyone would always be expected to have endless faith on laws. Wise people (and a bit of rich as well) would try always to talk in two ways: with soft words or through a legal notice.

Now a tale of two cities, in one of the city there were hundred cases of theft in a month and in all the hundred cases, the culprit was caught. In the other city, there were ten case of theft in a month and in only one case, the culprit was caught. Which city was more ordered at that time?

The joyability of the third party laws would never remain just giving punishments, but it is the orderness that together would provide entirety to its objectives in the outlooks of the people. For this, it would always remain dependent on other disciplines functioning properly. For long the discipline that takes help of the fear factor for itself would have to bear with the fear factor of her misuse rather than her use in the hands of other disciplines. Till then, laws can plan for getting rid off its virginity.

As far as reforms are concerned true and talented lawyers would be the most valuable resource for any kind of reformation.

In laws, more complex laws and more parallel punishment will help in refining its objectives. Experiments should be welcomed.

6.5.5 Economics:

For a developing nation like ours, possessing all the qualities and quantities of becoming a superpower, 'superpowerness', ultimately would be an attribute more related to the consistency of security that her systems can provide to her citizens rather than that to the variables of economics. India's GDP was about 20% that of the world when British came to India, though what were their intentions that I think God knows better, and roughly it takes about fifty years in converting Economics into full proof security. And this time in the worst case it won't be human beings of any kind. It would be robots, microbes and radiations.

The genetic endowment of the British and now of their true colonies as well, may be suspected for their typical way of doing business. But, now we need not to worry about anything, as the world as few of intelligent British Colonizers might have wished has become a comparatively civilized place for doing business. We need not to worry about even for the worst case. Till ours GDP would be 20% that of the world, the British Colonizers and their true colonies would be enjoying somewhere in the Andromeda. May be they would be busy in a war with the aliens.

The genetic endowment of the British and now of their true colonies as well, may also be suspected for their typical way of caring for other civilizations and as the supplier of the superior knowledge. But again nothing to worry about, as the world, as few of them had wished, has become a very civilized place for sharing knowledge as well. Their true and honest logics are still working for us in a remote sense.

So by and large there is no threat from any of the civilized businessmen or any of the knowledge masters but there are threats from the ignorant that are still far from being civilized in any sense.

As far as only economists are concerned they are working well. In fact they work well in every age. The people are enjoying their ideas of capitalism now the higher education would like to enjoy their ideas of venture capitalism.

As far as the understandings towards Economics are concerned first it would be the joyability of the Chanakyamen to understand the Smithmen. For searching better ways of using modern theories, it would be the joyability of hypothesis to understand observance. It would be the joyability of systems to understand the disciplines first. It would be the joyability of the dreams to understand the realities first. Rest would be the joyability of the aliens.

Getting Focused: Fundamental Sciences would remain crucial for solving the problems and planning for general decisions. The sooner the world would forgot them, the sooner it would come to an end and hence the problems. The unification of knowledge would be expected to have the most wondering of the applicabilities. The true joy would not be there in unifying the knowledge but in disunifying, materializing and exhausting it, for it main aim. Interesting. For this the collection of knowledge of history in a disciplined manner would be necessary and a complex systems approach would be expected to make it potentially sufficient for solving problems in a more satisfactory manner. Systems approach would help in gradually getting focused within a particular discipline with a hope of getting disciplines as stronger as feasible, their better understanding, its dispersal and better coordination among various disciplines.

6.6 Social System Development Model:

Social system development model or say discussion model would be the model that can be consumed for the reformations of the social systems. It would not be the way things would go, but the way things are going, would be partially depicted this way. The model in its simplest initial form would have three phases of development namely: systems engineering, analysis and design. The implementation details (unexpected to normal to expected case execution details) would be covered in the design phase. And the real execution phase is dash lined and covered by implementation details because of its fuzzy or non-

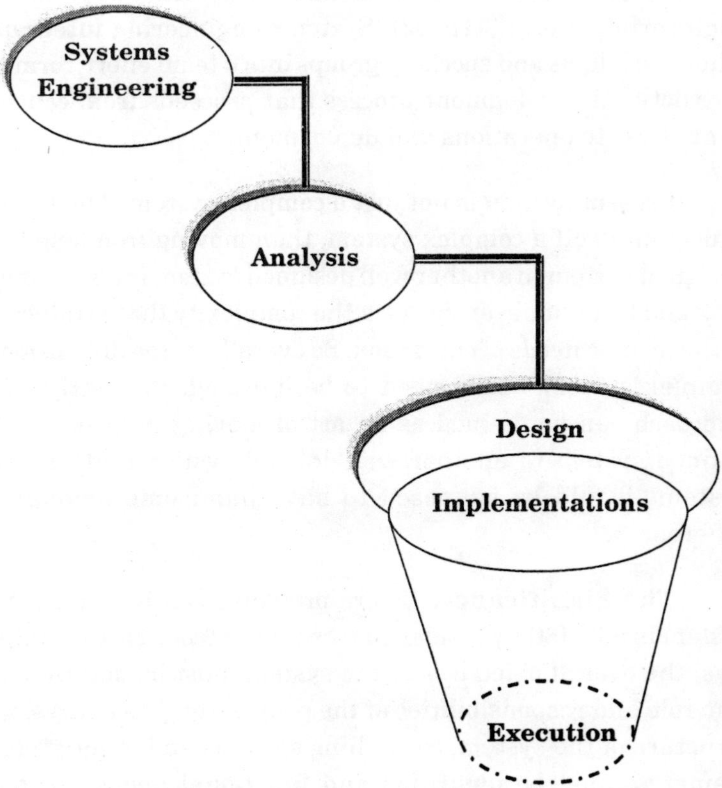

Fig. 5. Social System Development Model

deterministic nature just like that of human behavior and would lie somewhere in the implementation details. Simple intent: our neural network needs to be as dynamic and as brutal for the problems as the problems are themselves. Any general idea for solving problems would have super cascading effects. The following are the irksome details:

6.6.1 Phase-I: Systems Engineering

The Definition: Systems engineering is an interdisciplinary approach meant for enabling the realization and deployment of successful systems [INC02]. It can be viewed as the application of engineering techniques to the engineering of systems, as well as the application of systems approach to engineering efforts [THO03]. Systems engineering integrates other disciplines and specialty groups into a team effort, forming a structured development process that proceeds from concept to analysis to operations and deployment.

Present system is not just a complex system. The higher education itself a complex system, then moving from one well designed system to another well designed system is also a tough task and last but never the least the complexity that is inherent to the diverse needs of our nation. So overall a three dimensional complex system would need to be handled. Presently, this approach can be defined as an art of moving from one well-defined system to another well-defined system and the two systems would be supposed to have handsome amount of differences.

The Significance: Before problems can be solved, the system in which they reside must be understood. To accomplish this, the overall objectives of the system must be determined. The role and responsibilities of the people, the procedures, the structure of the system, controlling systems and other system elements must be identified and functional needs must be elicited, analyzed and modeled [RSP01]. The importance of systems engineering process would lie in the fact that it provides a platform start to the process of solving problem by initiating the process of understanding.

The Steps: The systems engineers would suppose to have a considerable knowledge of the system and its necessities before communicating in the details with the human resource elements of the system. They would have to have a feel of the roles, responsibilities and authority of the people on their own shoulders to have a better and clear picture of how the necessities would be fulfilled in the later phases of development. For understanding problems an approach for following problems is needed first. Now every small problem is influenced directly or indirectly by broader disciplines. The necessities would be analyzed to have a feasible forethoughts that will be needed further.

The Outcome: After the objectives, more detailed operational necessities would be identified by observance and discussion. Finally, the necessities would be analyzed to assess their clarity, completeness and consistency and a specification of the necessities and a system model would be created and validated.

The System Elements: To fulfill its role a system needs to depend on a variety of system elements, which together defines the overall system. These elements may be [RSP01]:

- **People** : The roles, responsibilities and the authorities.
- **Documentation** : Descriptive information that depicts the operations of the system.
- **Procedures** : The steps that define the execution of various operations at higher level of abstraction.

- **Controlling Elements** : The external systems that decide the various rules and regulations of the system, are responsible, and authorized for planning and implementation of the changes influencing the system under consideration.

- **Database** : A large, organized collection of information related to the various operations of the system, the behavior of the system, the static and dynamic information related to the various system elements as per the necessities.

From educational point of view some broader ideas would be:

- The study over the various needs of education system: philosophy, disciplines, contents, quantity, approach of study, examination etc.

- The study of general requirement and factor fulfilling them.

- The problems and the factors influencing the system.

- Study, discussion and documentation over research and plans of various institutes.

- Conducting seminars, workshops and field studies. Though a lot of document would be available in form of books and reports but still would need a revival for the young.

- Preparation of an activity model. Application of this model for large scale.

- Study and preparation from education models of various other nations. This would need a similar approach of studies for history of other nations and their history and present of education. Simple.

- Preparation of an abstract of overall higher education from various related aspects.

6.6.2 Phase-II: Analysis

The Definition: The term analysis can be defined as an abstract separation of a whole into its constituent parts in order to study the parts and their relations. Analysis in the development of system would be the process of more detailed study of various system elements and their relationship with each other, identification of patterns and generalizations.

The Significance: The significance of the process of analysis lies in depicting 'what' needs to be done. It would use a combination of textual and diagrammatic form to depict necessities for information, function and behavior in a way that is relatively easy to understand and more straightforward to review for correctness, completeness and consistency [RSP01]. The process of analysis would increase the overall understanding of the system, its functionalities to be performed, and the objectives to be met within the system.

The Steps: Analytical studies would help in learning the independent strength of the elements and holistic studies would help in finding the short and long interdependence among the elements. The information, functional and behavioral necessities would be modeled. The following guidelines would need to be followed iteratively for understanding and depicting the various necessities:

- Represent the information domain of the necessities.

- Define the functions to be performed by the system.
- Represent the behavior of the system (as consequences of external events).
- Feasibility studies from financial, political, legal, psychological, regional, cultural, behavioral, managerial, technological etc. perspectives. The various angles of studies would be difficult to generalize and would depend obviously on the problem under consideration.
- Finding alternatives.

With the approach of systems engineering it would be more about studying a problem and then thinking about the subjects influencing the efforts towards solution. Certainly it's more natural to our problem solving activities.

- The analytical process should move towards implementation details.

The Outcome: The work product of the analysis phase would include the detailed description of various system elements, their functionalities, relationship among them, flow of information and control through the system represented in form of diagrams or models for providing a better understanding. In other words, an understanding and pictorial representation of 'what needs to be done'. And it is not like that many new activities would be performed, but in a more clear manner by making things more easily visible.

Again from educational view some ideas are like:

- Daily life-cycle of people involved in the system: students, teachers and parents.
- The disciplinary purpose: profession, system, and awareness.

- The different professions: nature, skills and knowledge orientation, growth. Daily life-cycle of workers. The types of customers or end users attached with the profession.
- The different degree courses: their connectivity with different professions.
- The different degree courses: their contents, significance and the dependencies on them.
- The different approach of curriculum development.
- The different ways of examinations.
- Statistics and growth rate regarding courses and professions and figures related to higher education.
- Study over three broader perspectives: research, profession and vocation with keeping research at prime priority.
- Study over 'why' and 'how' 9-10% graduates are employable.
- Study over illiterate people upto various ages.
- Preparation of the set of various solutions and alternatives.

6.6.3 Phase-III: Design

The Definition: Design is a meaningful engineering representation of something that is to be built. It is like a blue print of the problems [RSP01].

The Significance: The significance of the design phase lies in specifying 'how' to perform 'what' have been decided in the analysis phase. It would focus more on listing the solution and alternatives with priorities and their implementation details.

The Steps: The major steps in the design phase would involve the reformation of the various system elements as per the necessities. The system would be defined in terms of flow of information, control, funds or whatever entities are there. Validation policies would be made and the new systems elements would be examined on the basis of different criteria. The old analytical components would be fitted with the new ones and then different components would be reorganized to give a complete solution.

The Implementation Details: Just to begin implementation details would be covered in the design phase. It would cover the worst, unexpected to normal to expected and best case execution details. Every step would need to be very clear from various relevant aspects of finance, administration, behaviour, answerability so that people related to implementation can understand things with minimum investment of their time and intelligence.

Design would be the documents of various ideas along with their requirements for implementing them. A number of general alternatives would depend on the issues of finance and availability of human resource.

For our education system, after two to three year of study and analysis things would be pretty clear. The system may move back to the old 9 + 2 model for adding one more year to higher education so as to make it more relevant for today's requirement. This may also help us in building the double helix of educational values and educational applications through education in every domain. As far as useless competitive exams

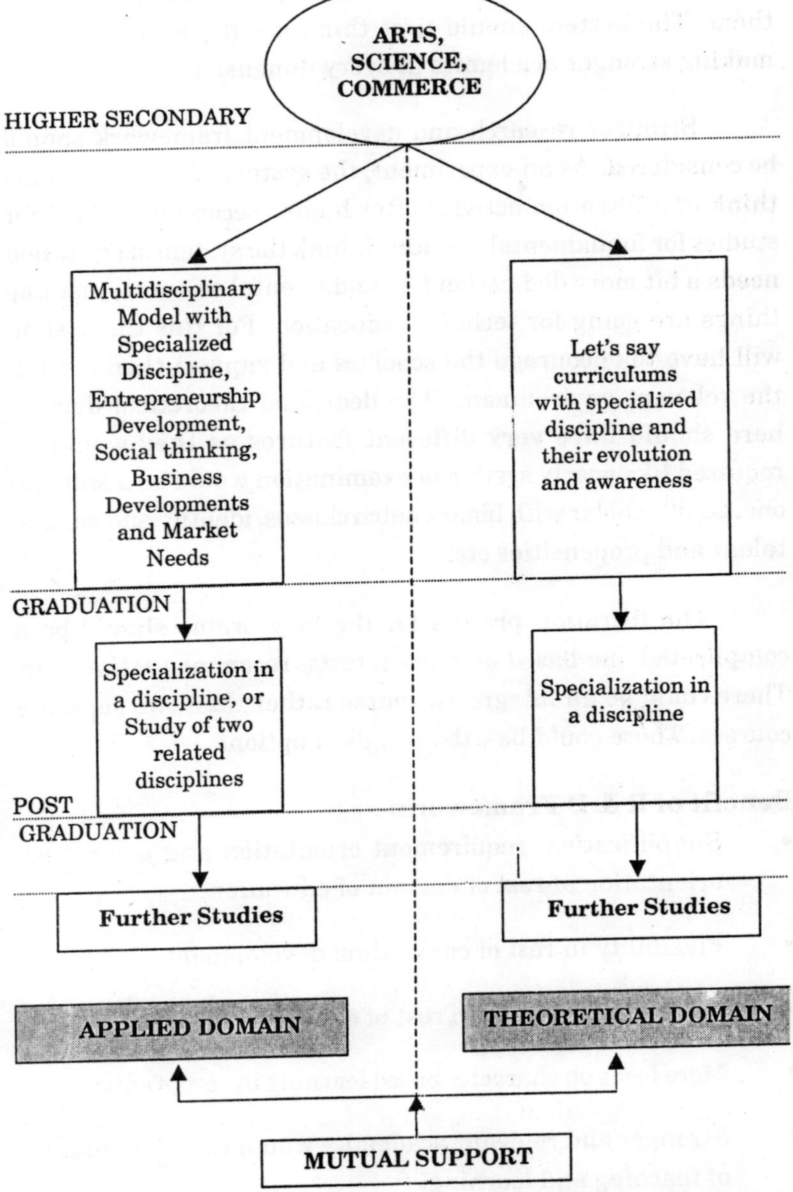

Fig: 6 The Bifurcated System of Higher Education : A Possibility

are concerned our academics would need to learn a lot from them. The system should first think of all possible ways of making stronger academics in every dimension.

Stronger research and development framework should be considered. As an experiment, the system of education may think of a filtration activity after higher secondary school for studies for fundamental sciences. I think the system of education needs a bit more dedication for fundamental sciences, just like things are going for technical education. For this the system will have to encourage the scholars and support them within the relevant environment. The dedicated theoretical domain here should have very different features as they would be required like yearly system of examination would be a suitable one, 25-30 scholar with binary batch classes, identify and sustain talent and propensities etc.

The filtration process for the lazy brains should be a complicated one based on marks, tests, recommendations etc. There could be an integrated course rather than two separate courses. There could be...thousands of options.

Benefit of R & D Framework:

- Simplification, requirement orientation and awareness orientation of rest of domain of education.
- Flexibility in rest of curriculum development.
- Experimentation with rest of education system.
- More focus on character based learning in rest of education.
- Stronger and relevant academics would result in quality of teaching and learning.
- Quality of research. More efficient utilization of resources.

- Savings of unnecessary and over distributed scientific resources.
- Better platform for research scholars.
- Satisfactory.
- Would make sure that ISRO's "Mangalyaan" won't land on my terrace.
- For finishing work pending in physics.
- Something that our education and education people purely deserves.

Potential Threat: HR attrition.

Potential Solution: Experimentation, Intelligent 'in-waste-ment' of money initially, emotions, anecdotes and wait and watch.

Few applicable points:

- Scholars, it's not that era now. It's not the 17th century. Opportunities lost once in science means opportunities lost forever.
- Scholars, the duties of our Universities for next 100 years is not to get into list of the top 100 or 500, but to serve the masses only. Major research would be only that that underlies the applications for near and far future.
- Scholars, scientific infrastructures are not the household utensils made in Indus valley civilization so that they can be brought out by digging the earth. By the grace of God, we are no less than 1200 million people (We should always thank God for his lazy engineering habits that kids don't happen in a month or two) who are still waiting

for many things. Our foremost joyability with the knowledge and its applicability would be to serve our people. There are millions of small children who still do not have the opportunity to attend even the primaries of the education. So it's our duty to make the best out of the higher ones.

- And wise investors, kids are very smart now. You can't impress them for just being curious and imaginative. Every middle school scholar knows that Peter Higgs propounded the concept of higgs boson some 60 years back and more than 5000 scientists are engaged since last 20 years in search of the truth, spending millions of rupees and at present the machine is out of order. Hierarchical systems can be considered over flat systems from human resource perspectives.

- Combining teaching and research to a greater extent, I don't think would be feasible in short-term. Something important- infrastructure, money, time, relevance in the two, lack of resources, requirement of research, limitations to the level to which work can be refined and modularized, would always be missing. Still deep thinking and more deep thinking and more on this matter needs to be there. Some sort of *'jugat lagani hogi'* with long term plans.

- Respect brain at each possible step.

- Money should be utilized with human resource at top priority and second in keeping things clean and dust free.

- The eccentric's dens should be cultured with a sequential plan based on the science of mental life and patience. Now as Research Projects are more team work oriented and long term ventures so curriculums needs to be developed from this point of view with inclusion of disciplinary awareness and philosophy of work around anecdotes.

- Now the upcoming era, forever, would be about optimizing things rather then finding new theories.
- Now as we have started making few bugs so first we should plan for making strong fundamental planning and fundamental management.

Benefits of Multidisciplinary Curriculums:

- When it is not sure (for anyone) in what nature of work domain a scholar will land exactly.
- More widespread and relevant thinking.
- Balance of values and utility of education.
- Multidisciplinarity at the right time.
- Curriculums with multiple employments focus.
- Quality in teaching and learning.
- Self-learning capabilities.
- Inclusion of personal management, work management.
- Flexibility in curriculum development.

Where employability is required managerial approach can be preferred. Where social thinking is needed social sciences and awareness can be preferred. But one thing that needs to be kept in mind is that the work process and specially decision making can be coupled around a single discipline only, so better orientation of disciplinary studies and documents regarding work needs to be there with prime importance. All this development would need a systems approach.

Few applicable points:

- Employability should be preferred over always. Higher education should not be utilized for the purpose of social service. Self-learning and designing skills should be encouraged. Connectivity, orientation and co-ordination would be the keywords.

- Teacher's academic institutes could be preferred over teachers training institutes.

- Giving just opportunities are just not sufficient. Those who have turned opportunity into achievements could be praised in material terms.

- The core philosophy of education needs to be changed. Now development is over. All is about how things can be managed, what needs to be managed and how well all this can be done. Balancing between various factors would be expected: value and utility, philosophy and reality, being and resource, history and present, gravity and ready-awareness, staticness and dynamism etc.

- System Information/Process Engineering, System Information/Process Maintenance, System Service Documentations, Business Information/Process Engineering, Business Information/Process Maintenance, Business Service Documentations should be encouraged. Now as different philosophies are quite mature and what majorly we need is planning and maintenance, so a problem solving approach from the very beginning can be considered. The different approach can be cultured around available systems and businesses around us. The importance of these approaches would be realized by scholars after ten years of leaving the education system.

- Changing the name of degree from B.A., B.Sc., B.Com to B.M.S (Bachelor Of Multidisciplinary Studies) (Main discipline) wherever required would give more flexibility in redesigning curriculums and would let things free from a lot of unnecessary arguments.

- Approach of studies and approach of examinations would solve most of the problems.

- Scholars, higher education is not about spoon-feeding. Grab the opportunities to the best. Gradually should turn into an autonomous learner. Don't ask what higher education has given to us just think what we can give to higher education. There would be a trade off between accountability of the system and flexibility to enjoy the freedom of learning. So young would have to compensate for the accountability on their shoulders.

- Higher education shouldn't be about personal development of kids but it should be like an agreement between society and them. No one is supposed to take care of higher education. Higher education is supposed to take care of itself and everyone else. Higher education is more about making a good worker out of a good being.

- Requirement oriented systems though won't be able to match idealistic standards immediately but would satisfy system in material terms and would help in moving towards perfection. Higher education is about telling the scholars every neutral reality: nothing wrong and nothing right.

- Money for all this should come as directly as possible from the pockets of the people and should go as first voluntarily in the pockets of the teachers (with clear cut more defined roles, if possible, the real time projects, may be certification courses) and then for keeping things clean and dust free. We can have partly post-paid higher education scheme, we can have money-back policy based on certain criteria. We can search on internet for more ideas.

- Subjects with disciplinary orientations like for business and systems would be more affordable and effective than interdisciplinary courses.

- Don't provide too much free of cost quality.

Benefits of the Old 9 + 2 model:

- Saving of one year of resources.

- Space for multidisciplinarity, ethical and awareness studies at the right age.

- Lesser and right burden on school going kids.

- Maintaining importance of specialization.

For professional courses the one-year can be used for:

- Separating competitions exams from academics exams:

  - Lesser burden on kids.

  - Quality of higher academics.

  - Right focus on school academics.

  Or

For more and the needed space for professional courses:

- Work management, professional and application orientation.
- Quality of academic discipline.
- Quality of work in profession.

Or

For both: fifty-fifty.

Few applicable points:

- Curiosity could be engaged mainly in search of the ethical universe outside and within.
- More emphasis should be given on learning of mathematics
    - Physical.
    - General.
    - Applicable.
    - Experiments.
- The brains of kids should not be considered as a hard disk of 80 GB but as a RAM of 256 MB.
- Avoid too much of experimentation with the education system. Say no to artificial ways of curiosity and imagination. Natural development is not supposed to support education but education is supposed to support the natural development of the learners.
- Quantity of education should not only decide the quality of education. Consistency and the approach of efforts are very important.

- Refining knowledge is very important but should be imposed minimum on the education system.

- For a full freedom for imagination and curiosity of scholars a better and complete central control would be a must.

- More emphasis on the ethics and morals is not because of there is dearth of it but more of it would result in more dedication towards scientific studies resulting in more revenues and more GDP. Happiness should come and should come as a byproduct.

These are some ideas but not the only ideas. Lot of ready-made ideas are available in the market. Simply, consider and corner them. Lot of complexities are also there. In case of any dilemma stick to experiments.

6.6.4 Understanding Systems Engineering:

It may be named differently, something like 'System Ingeniouring' - leave no discipline behind. Ingeniouring = the discipline dealing with the art or science of applying scientific knowledge to practical problems cleverly. To begin with this dynamic science would need comprehensive knowledge and understanding of Science. Then would need a minimum of four years of regular studies in an academic environment. And simply it could be a simple representation of any case in terms of answers of few basic questions: 'why?', 'what?', 'how?', 'who?', 'where?', 'when?' and 'till when?' The studies can be organized in form of a master's degree like "Master of System Developments in higher education".

The best way to understand systems engineering would be 'philosophy and execution going hand in hand'. First learning the theme of the theory and then finding it in the practical.

That would enrich theoretical concepts and then practical would be felt at comparative ease. And so on.

As a part of parallel process along with the normal forward engineering process, reverse engineering process, would provide a much better understanding. Especially, when financial and behavioral feasibility become major factors for implementations the reverse engineering process would help a great deal in deciding priorities and saving lot of time and effort.

The approach of system engineering as such is very complex for artificial systems but for this purpose its main motto would be to develop analytical abilities and understanding, proper representation and managing the complexity of a system involving human roles and responsibilities. There would be different aspects for system approach: designing a system, understanding behavior of system, their relationship with each other, moving from one system to another and moving from problem statements to solutions. For understanding a system and its different features in a way or other the matured sciences dealing with this art are already their like complex systems theory, systems thinking etc. Together with an engineering approach it would be about application on present scenario at general as well as specialized level. System oriented learning and system science are not much related.

Systems approach may be cursed for its lack of clarity. Yet it is fruitful. Simply, avoid over generalizations, avoid over-refinement, always learn with cases, solve simple problems first, keep handsome general awareness, always learn with a domain under consideration. Think in as simple terms as possible. Generalize less, know more. Watch less of television. Rest *'Haule Haule'* anyone would fall in love with System Ingeniouring - leave no discipline behind. Read this book twice and then throw it in the Ganges.

Some unsmooth key features about the engineering approach:

This approach is especially beneficial when the majority of dreams are as *'haseen'* as those of *'Mr. Mungerilal'*, when opportunities are there *'Chappar phade ke'*, when majority of the ideals and majority of the standards are made rightly by majority of the aliens and majority of people are in a right major impression by that majority of aliens, when there in majority all the need and in majority not at all the possibility to realize the majority of those standards and still the majority of the people are not satisfied with what majority they have and also when the majority of the efforts of the majority of the state can be called as unsatisfactory in majority, when the state would always have to satisfy all of the stated limits:

- One world one philosophy. Who the hell is trying to maintain this earth at 3 levels of abstraction when it is supposed to work at 5 levels of abstractions?

- When dialogue, understanding, and discussion are at top priority.

- Enjoyment of work. The first and foremost requirement for education reforms.

- One time investment for development. Generations till eternity would enjoy it.

- The first and foremost right on education would be of the student.

- Should not be considered as a way of thinking, but a way of providing services to the people.

- Complicated but comprehensible, complex yet clear, unrestricted yet disciplined, heavy yet manageable.

- At present science of mental life should be kept at the top of each and everything and then education then should come the State and the Statesmen. After some 2-3 decades, education can be planned to be at the top.

- There won't be any better alternative of the state for next 100 years.

- Helpful state-of-the-art methodology would work for the planning for getting rid of the helpless art of the state. Metropolitan cities can be considered as guinea pigs for performing experiments as a virtual nation. Believe in Democracy, don't be a nut about it ways. Keep on experimenting and experimenting and experimenting but for just next two centuries.

- Human level best.

- When ideas are saturated but resources are lacking. This approach would help in proactive planning.

- So far, cardiac muscle fibers cannot substitute for neurons and dendrites.

- Nothing harm in knowing more (provided you are paid for it).

- Knowledge of different disciplines would help further in refining a particular discipline.

- Not just knowing more but bringing applicability out of it.

- The approach can be utilized by the government for providing redefined stated limits and supervising the sector of higher education in case of its independent regulation for whole or for part.

- More of knowledge would lessen the need of mechanistic thinking and would keep up the importance of value of knowledge first for the person owning it. It needs to be sure that no one is making a machine out of any one: a balance of human being and human resource, a balance of value and utility.

- Why it is important to know about history and why it is important not to fall in love with it.

- Respect for other perceptions.

- Brain, power and money would need to fall in love with each other.

- The disciple would be good in arguments - 'One eyed in a group of blinds'.

- The disciple would be - 'Jack of all and master of one'.

- The disciple would take for time for arriving at conclusions but the conclusions would be conclusions.

- An alternative (better alternative itself would provide).

- Knowing things not just with the intent of knowing them but moving them as well.

- Why it is important to listen to all before making your own decision.

- Truth doesn't exist in terms of poems. Still, why it's important to understand it in terms of poems and why majority should understand it in terms of poems.

- Why creating too much of brains of this kind is not needed.

- Would keep anyone's CPU busy and would keep it cool. One of the most fundamental principles of computer science.
- When chances of changes are rarest.
- Why everyone should understand everyone else.
- Providing an artificial touch to the natural process of division of labor.
- How much a person should know and when it's good to take help of consultants.
- It won't be a feeling that something has been earned but something was missing and it has come back and a lot is still missing.
- Limitation of human thinking process.
- Cutting down unnecessary energy and emotions.
- Why it's important to take care of everyone.
- The world is not what it is. It becomes. Rather it's made. Ideally, it should become.
- Trust in the decisions on which generations would depend. Honesty should deal at 'personal', but when it would come to 'system' level finally knowledge would come to help.
- Within limited amount of resources why it's important to think from requirement perspectives with an engineering approach.
- Why thinking exactly about the standard made by others would not be possible. Why similar ideas would turn into different details.

- Theoretically very simple: There are disciplines and there is an interdisciplinary approach.

- Why present should not be charged for damages of history (When there is failure to conclude over anyone responsible, things should be imposed to someone in history.)

- Not just about knowing 'what is right' and 'what is wrong', but also 'what is going to happen' and 'what not'.

- There is no dearth of quality standards available on this earth but there would be dearth of resources. More population is not just more human resource but more problems as well. Engineering first scans over the availability of resources then it deals with the quality standard and what are the parameters involved in realizing that standards.

- Politics after proper documentation.

- Reality is distorted form of ideality.

- Ideality should be defined ideally and feasibly.

- It's not like that how much luxury is available in market but how much money is there in anyone's pocket.

- Y money is important, Y it is always less, Y it is difficult to make it, Y majority should make it and make it more and more.

- More scientific, less human dependent, less dependent on factors of intelligence, experience, wisdom and personal perceptions.

- If disciplines are considered as narrowly defined, how broadly a subject could be defined with the maintenance of human understanding.

- What are the limits to interdisciplinarity? What all could be the applicability of interdisciplinary studies?
- Better and self-management of intellectual and disciplinary conflicts.
- When the sequences of decisions and the makers of decisions are more crucial than the decision themselves.
- Understanding problems resulting out of the non-evolutionary division of mental labor.
- It's important to understand that world is an entity which is moving from one state to another, at the same time it's important to understand that generations to come should not be confused.
- The moment a thought would come the amount of evolutionary and real time knowledge in the mind would create a design with it is implementation feasibilities.
- It's not about new ideas but about leaving no idea, and more important the sequencing of the application of the ideas. And as far as original ideas involving the infrastructure of pen and paper is concerned, I don't think anything is left.
- A better way of transferring knowledge from one civilization to another.
- The movement in any direction would need a lot of safety valves in-between, between the two rivals of idealism and realism.
- Can be consumed for moving from socially and legally cruel governments to scientifically and logically cruel governments.

- Simplest way to unify knowledge with immediate applicability.
- Easily modified to particular requirements.
- Convergent thinking of various segments of society.
- Making the most out of division of labor.
- Providing building blocks and building logics rather than buildings.
- Efficient approach: minimum need for new disciplines.

Some more abstract features about the engineering approach:

- Special approach not a generic concept
- Dynamic
- Systemic Study
- Real Time Thinking
- Result Oriented
- World View To Specific View
- Complexity Management
- Problem Centric
- System Oriented
- Requirement Oriented
- Logic Based
- Thinking From Multiple Orientation
- Replicative
- Developmental
- Futuristic
- Holistic
- Experimentalism
- Realistic Thinking
- Satisfactory
- Application Oriented
- Self-developing
- Spontaneous
- Chaos Handling
- Knowledge Based
- Understanding At Level Of Abstraction
- Sustainable

6.6.5 Phase IV: The Execution

No system is perfect. Every system for its success largely would depend on humans. Humans are capable of compensating the weakness of a system by their hard work. Humans can also take personal benefits because of the flaws a system have. Before designing systems the engineer would be supposed to have good knowledge of human behavior, psychology, their personal needs and every other direct factor that may alter the normal execution of the system.

For systems other than higher education this comprehensive approach may not be needed, but as in our nation problems are highly interdependent and would need a very long term planning, so rethinking about the systems with this approach could be a better option. People with enough experience in the particular domain can think of moving ahead with this systems approach of thinking. Though systems approach for solving problems would be nothing new and is something that is quite natural to us, still the presentation would need to be made simple enough so that the understanding that it generates can be easily shared with the people who have no conscious idea about it. Any theory should be developed in the interest of the common people and it will be good if they could have direct stake in the process of understanding and defining problems.

Finally, reformation of heavy loaded education system would be as simple as repairing a wing of a plane in the clouds or an open-heart surgery of a human foetus or like filling air in the tyre of an unstoppable moving vehicle. Patience would be the key to success.

The Planning: So, know a little about different discipline and hence the world, the nation and the people and then study according to the need of the domain under consideration. The worldview can be designed according to the domain under consideration. The more important are the principles the far more important is the contemporary world of immense worldwide contests where economy plays a vital role and even governments would like to invest in profitable business and so should be the case. For larger scale quality in education is highly interrelated phenomenon with quality of higher education all the way heuristically related to the quality of primary education. But concentration should be mainly on higher education. For a complex system like that of higher education certainly the knowledge base needs to be very heavy and can be supplied with:

System-oriented curriculum:

1. Good understanding of major disciplines.
2. System Specific Knowledge.
3. Systems engineering approach.

Initially experiment with:

1. Young computer science graduates.
2. 8-10 years experienced teachers.

And don't wish that these people should be remembered by generations to come. They should live and think as common people. Why here emphasis should be given on young because they remain closest to real time problems, academic environment, because of their inquisitive nature because of less of knowledge and less of experience. Also as education reforms would be a process that would run for certain decades, so it is important to search a school of thought that would combine the gravity of the olds with the dynamism of the young.

Finally, all this would need proper stuffs for marketing and entertainment. Interested people should know every reason behind the reformations. Interested people should know every reason behind every success and behind every failure.

Lord Macaulay If Then Else Institute of Systems Ingeniouring For Evolutionary Justice Through Learning and Education (LMITEISIEJTLE), near Neori village, Lalghati,

Bhopal. My M.P. Govt. is very generous and experienced for donating land for social causes so I hope that that won't be a big problem also I don't think that she would be able to afford about 20-25 such institutes, also a small name could be searched. I hope that thought would come up worth enough to be considered further as an mundanely authorized and publicly paid business in form of an institute as this source code for the system of higher education if found executable may give a very strong possibility to lead to the reformation of the overall system of education in too far future. And any establishment, whatsoever, with all its aspects must come strictly under the guidance, direction and leadership of the highest spirits of higher education of the nation that is the University Grants Commission (UGC) in our case. The task of our UGC should be restricted to signing grant cheque or we will change its name to something like Indian Institute of Universal Learning (IIUL) and would let her decide her extent of universality. Also words like 'Commission' and 'Council' should be avoided as they give impressions of temporariness and ephemerality. Every institute with whatsoever administrative capacity and executive authority she might have, should have some daily doses of curiosity, imagination and absurdity, that is, kids and young around to every extent of feasibility.

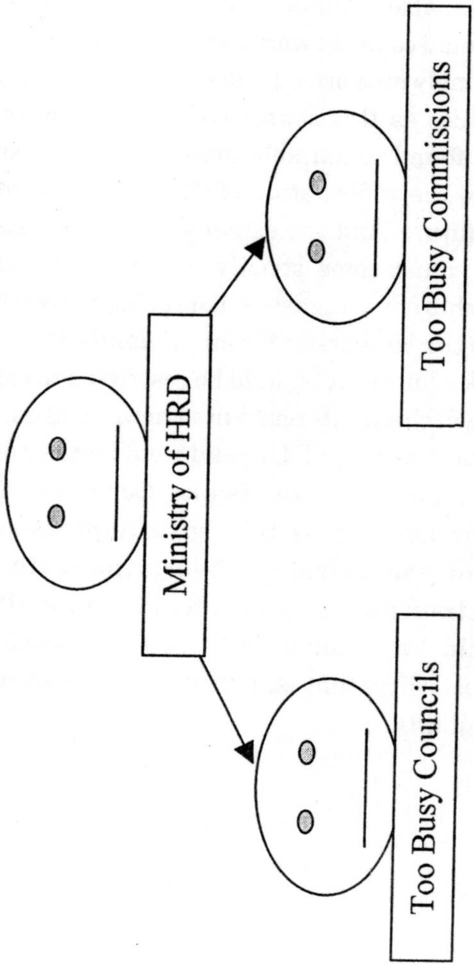

At Present : Something like this is existing and something like this is natural and something like this is going to remain till eternity.

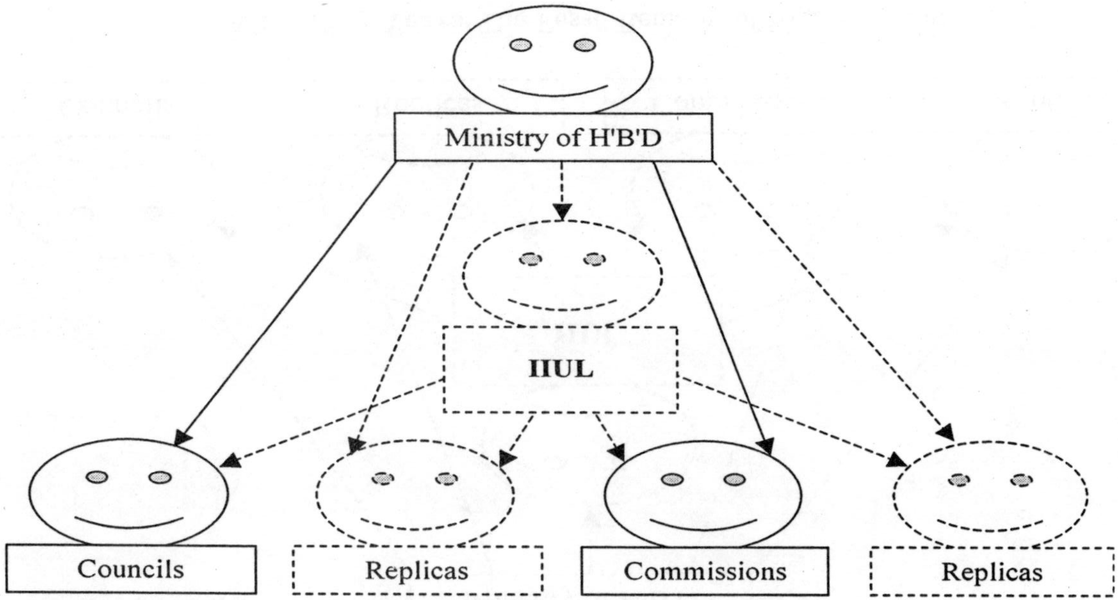

Futurology: Something like this would be needed in near future and something like this is artificiality for moving towards more of naturalness and something like this is not going to remain there till eternity.

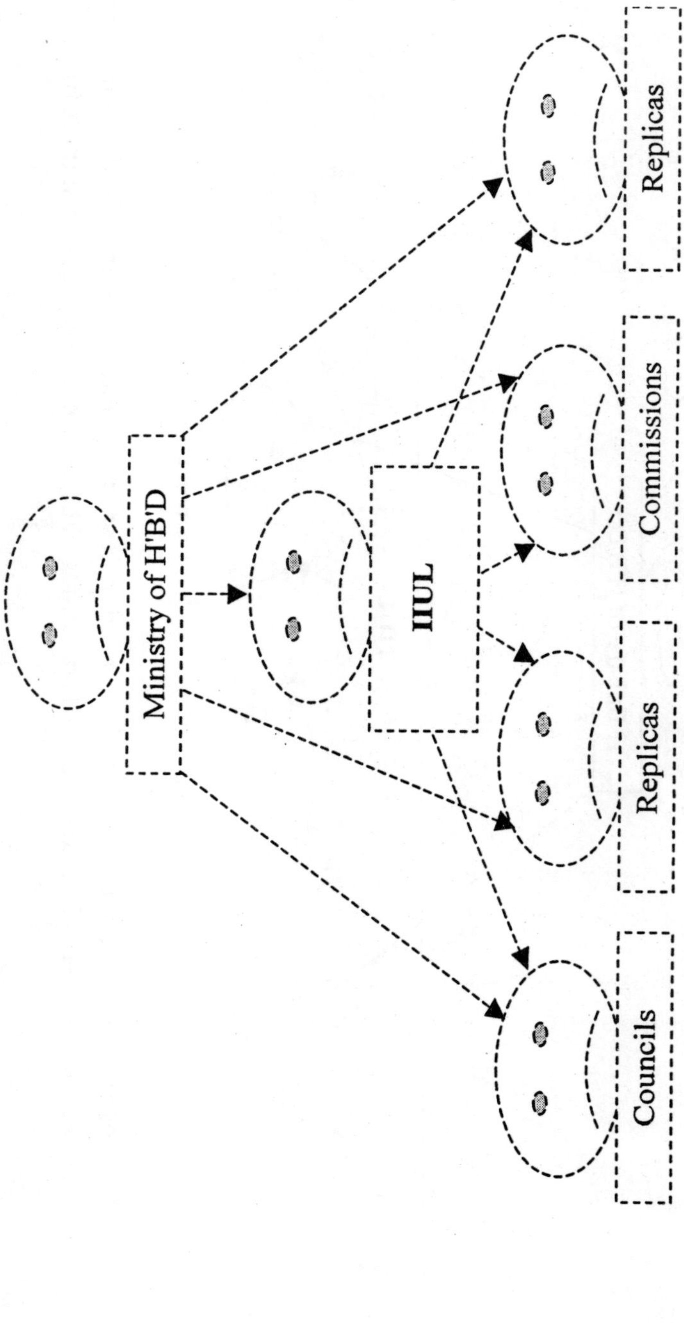

After Fifty Years: The Fossil Remains of Higher Education.

7

Thinking Thoughts

"The search for the truth is more precious than its possession"
- Albert Einstein

7.1 Thinking Thoughts: When Imagination meets Programming

Einstein has further said - "These thoughts did not come in any verbal formulation. I rarely think in words at all. A thought comes, and I may try to express it in words afterward."

Thoughts are very stubborn in nature. When they would come, from where they would come, that they would decide only. We can say a thought comes from somewhere, at sometime and then it is expressed in words. Now going again from these words to this 'somewhere' and at that 'sometime', is a very interesting job.

Learning from thoughts would lead to interdisciplinary aerobics of the dendrites. Again it would be a less tiresome way of understanding problems and needs than that from the skeleton theories or by imprisoning words in a rectangle, square, rhombus, parallelogram, ellipse, circle or whatsoever it is. Also it is importance to understand the figures as closely related to the ideas as possible. Like the doughnut shape of the logical awareness model reflects the unification of knowledge and would make sure that we have confined the ideas to a certain extent and no idea shallow or deep, general or special would be out of the reach. The details of the following ideas would be discussed later on.

7.1.1 Religion, Faith, God......

01. I think the most typical fear to get rid of is not that of God, but that of his bureaucrats.

02. Faith upto the penultimate level of refinement is a set of assumptions based on empiricism and empiricism based on set of assumptions. To the last level it is simply faith.

03. Religion in my opinion is a diamond that is being utilized by many as a piece of coal since ages. In the minds of the people, it should get rid of misconceptions, rigidness and irrationalism by the most democratic, meritocratic and scientific manner. And the mannerism should take care of the sentiments of the faithful devotees, so that they should not hold guilty of going against traditions and culture.

04. If interested in religious spiritualism, then be a non-possessive lover of mundane materialism.

05. True knowledge is not what takes us to salvation, but it is something that makes us humble and generous and initiates the process for salvation. After this initiation, rest of knowledge is a mechanism. True knowledge is meant for bringing us closer to the creation of God by creating and bringing a true human out of us and hence finally taking us closer to God.

06. Getting impressed first by human achievements is more important than by Gods achievements. We can learn better from the beings of our own kind, enjoying similar kind of privileges.

07. I think nature never remains in a position to forgive humans. This precious privilege is enjoyed by humans only and hence should be utilized sensibly.

08. We can manage without deities but not with devils.

09. Everyone does not have time to understand each and everything hence arisen the concept of faith.

10. We believe in God but rarely think about him.

11. God shows us the right way and for this, we can praise him but we would hardly take out some steps to walk that way.

12. "Knowledge belongs to the world, from where it comes ultimately. Its soul purpose is to serve mankind and humanity independent of any Religion, race, nation and region. Moreover, its true value lies in serving this purpose only". All this is rubbish. Put tax on the use of knowledge to each and every possible extent.

13. Religious thinkers are supposed to follow God and to have faith on Einstein while scientific thinkers are supposed to follow Einstein and to have faith on God.

14. Omnipotent God and karma philosophy are two contradictory phenomenons.

15. God is not an issue of senses; he is still a matter of hypothesis. Anything or anyone, real or hypothetical, if

making our things easier even phenomenally, should be inherited for further considerations.

16. Truly, no one leaves a Religion, but a set of mentalities.

17. Everyone who is helping us in coming closer to God is no less than a God for us.

18. We can always have faith on God's words, but whether the same is written in the books in the same mannerism is a matter of justification. Making others to follow our own words is common human intellectual psychology. To know self, we should know self, as life, as a human being is very precious.

19. Thinkers now should come up with timesaving thinking procedures and shortcut examples.

20. A man with lot of knowledge, but no respect for others is just like a mobile connection with lot of balance but no validity. At any juncture, the purpose of knowledge needs to be clear, not just it's systematic and classified assimilation. Such assimilation of knowledge is necessary for knowing its purpose but would never be sufficient.

21. Religion is an ocean of knowledge, first take a dip, find the pearls of simplicity, generosity, love and respect for all and then enjoy surfing the waves.

22. Life as a human being is very precious. Soul-searching is very important: what we are, what we want to be, how we would be, where we stands as compared to our ideals and role models. Having faith on God and Religion is important but being a blind follower or a bigot is good for no one.

23. Majority wants peace and happiness; only few want authorities and responsibilities.

24. Just love your God, rest is his job.

25. We change our self when we come to God or to a true saint. If we could remain what actually we are, then that would make God's and saint's job comparatively easier.

26. True knowledge is something that is useful for us all the time, even if others fail to make the best of it.

27. There is a very fundamental conceptual presentation mistake with two great Religions of Jainism and Hinduism and that is these institutions believe that we human beings pay for our *karmas*. The truth is that we all pay for our foolishness and negligence, some known to us and some not. We should believe in the euphemistic way of presenting the thoughts but not at the cost of the exact and the indispensable truth. God takes this form as the implementation details for making judgments.

28. We should avoid misusing the logical certainties of religious principles and thinking.

29. While finding solutions keep Religion aside. Because one problem with Religion is that it would always provide immediate solution for you.

30. God does not remain interested in principles. He remains interested in controversies. This world is definitely his plan.

31. Why to just help the poor? Why not to think of eradication of poverty as well?

32. Jainism = Science – Mathematics.

33. Religion = Politics – Answerability.

34. Democracy = Religion – Hell – Heaven.

35. Just take care of God's creations; he would take care of you.

36. Half-baked Religion and half-baked Spiritualism often lead to unconscious state of ignorance and egotism.

37. As far as Religion is concerned just keep one thing in mind that is God is far more smart than human beings: mathematically and scientifically, emotionally and politically, rationally and irrationally, cleverly and skillfully, humorously and dangerously, legally and argumentatively, 'UMLly' and 'OOPSly', 'ERDly' and 'DFDly', and 'SQLly' and 'JAVAly'.

38. Every civilization has the right to prosper with her own culture, in fact every civilization has the duty to prosper with her own culture.

39. Why to lead the world? Do something so that world can itself follow you.

40. Man extremizes; God optimizes.

41. Religion is best friend of common men. Philosophers need to be cautious of Religion. Common men need to be cautious of philosophers.

42. God has been trying to keep his knowledge at poetic level of abstraction and that's why his requirements are not clear.

43. God's *'karma'* taxation policies would make sure that he is far more brutal than humans, may be how far he is responsible for his world and its each and every being.

44. God is far more materialistic in his implementation details than human beings.

45. As said earlier, God is far smarter than human beings. He knows everything and tells us so little. He hides mathematical model of each and every aspects of life and nature and offers us simple poems. He use to play pranks with us and we generous humans use to praise him.

46. I don't know why Hinduism was so helpless in dividing we humans beings in a number of set but I think its the only Religion which first tries to understand us as a human beings and then accordingly starts its lessons and preaching. Hinduism carried on her shoulders the weaknesses of common human thinking and human psychology and had no option other than to provide an authentic touch to all these weaknesses, but for how long?

47. Time for neo-Hinduism.

48. We look for examples when God looks an example in us.

49. Books are the most useful creation of humans. Writers are the most useless creation of God.

50. I have faith in God; I have faith in God that he is not utilizing human beings as guinea pigs.

51. God used 0.01% of his brain in creating this Universe and the rest 99.99% was consumed in creating and spreading etymological differentiation of words about it.

52. Why God is taking so much of headache? Simple - 'empty head devils den' so its better to have an ache in it then an opportunity for a devil. All this for human beings.

53. After going through the 'evens' of your Religion do another job - find 'odds' of other Religions and then find how your Religion is greater than other Religions.

54. Putting Religion in education was not a difficult task all the way from year 1834 to around 1978. Anyone could have done it easily this way - 'Ask your dad to get a broadband Internet connection. Read a bit of C++ or Java and object oriented programming paradigm. Read different Religions available. Then create an object-oriented form of each and every Religion. Now find and create a more generic and a common Object Oriented Religion. Now refine it using examples and anecdotes from different Religions. And then the most important thing pretend as that you have done everything perfectly in one go and you are a poetic saint'. But unfortunately no one did it.

55. Religion: Don't expect too much from others else you will have to suffer. Devotee: expected too much from others and suffered. Devotee's conclusion: Religion knows truth. Let us praise it.

56. Macaulay's India visit was actually a part of the strategies of the Gods, specially the Indian ones. And this lawyer was not made by God for losing cases but to sit back and enjoy the proceedings.

57. Religion provides the most beautiful of the generalizations and the most misused as well.

58. Religion is the only discipline that provides perfect end-to-end plans. But unfortunately one end lies in the hell and the other in the heaven.

59. Religion is the smartest discipline in the sense that it finishes its encroachments on other disciplines in minimum number of words. System Ingeniouring would

encroach disciplines in as many words as possible. So Religion and System Ingeniouring would differ in terms of levels of abstraction and Religion would be a lazy and clever big brother of System Ingeniouring.

60. Majority remains interested in what was happening some 2000 years ago. Few remain interested in what happened some 200 years ago.

61. God has been experimenting with truth and we have taken him seriously.

62. After centuries of research, analysis and development, God found it impossible to design truth without loopholes and then finally he decided to take risk with the 'loop-holed' truth and gave a bit of his heart and brain to human beings. So taking risk while R & D is very important.

63. Religion would have taken some mere 5000 years for eradication of poverty. 10-12 % of poors would have been kept alive for paying tribute to respective Gods.

64. God was jealous of profoundness of Hinduism and he was also worried about his dominance. And then he created Manu - '*ek teer do shikar*. 'Manu could have easily overridden God's intention, he could have asked his dad to get a broadband Internet connection and then........

7.1.2 Science, Mathematics......

01. The truth of Physics, Einstein and Next Einstein: Einstein was a storyteller who knew a little bit of Mathematics. Next Einstein also would be a very smart storyteller but would have to have a group of consulting mathematicians that would be lured metaphysically and successfully by him for the formal justification of his stories. Ultimately, his stories will certainly entertain and unfortunately

threaten people, until the charge would be taken by the Next-Next Einstein and this is what now physics is all about. And……I don't think Next-Next Einstein would ever happen.

02. There is something special about the equation 1+1. That is, it always gives 2, under any circumstances. Therefore, nothing could be more honest and true on this earth than Mathematics and that is why we are becoming more and more dependent on it.

03. Things seem quite easier and obvious once they come out of chaos.

04. Only Science is scientific.

05. Now I think time has come for physicist to take rest. Machines will help us in coming near to the truth: a new horizon where imagination would meet programming.

06. We should not suffer from limitations of any domain whether Science or Religion.

07. Science is something like speed. With Religion, it becomes something like velocity.

08. Technology can be purchased but not knowledge and Science.

09. Mathematics becomes the sense of Science when things are out of the reach of human senses.

10. Research is all about the delays in finding excuses that will not work, until you find something workable for the world. But the excuses they would always work for you.

11. Information can be given but knowledge can be gained only. Technology can be purchased but Science can be searched only.

12. Hard work is like derivation of a mathematical formula. Smartness is like the formula itself. Over smartness is like asking the 'derivator' for telling you the formula.

13. Technology is by-product of Science. Science is by-product of curiosity.

14. Playing with variables is more important than playing with the constants.

15. Science: As much knowledge as many conclusions. In fact every God expect his followers to conclude according to their knowledge rest they should have blind faith on the respective Religion.

16. Systems engineering would soon replace physics. It would prove to be a better story-writing tool.

17. Majority remains interested in becoming a proton or a neutron. Hardly, we would find people interested in becoming 'pi mesons'.

18. I think it is very important to define and arrive at truth in terms of thoughts. The logical certainties for the arrival should be acceptable by common sense.

19. I don't think that the truth would be as impressive as we might be thinking of it. After reaching the truth we would think of better alternatives. We would put question mark on God's abilities of creating things. After all we are human beings.

20. News headlines after some fifty years: 'Physicist on indefinite hunger strike'. After some 150 years: 'Government to put ban on Mathematicians'.

21. What Religion wishes with effortless consciousness, Science achieves with unconscious efforts.

22. There can be only two kinds of searches: the search for the moral universe and the search for the material universe. The two universes rather the searches are complementary to each other.

23. Few Religious philosophers especially the Jain ones are the smartest consumers of Science. Where Religion comes in resonance with Science they would take help of Science for promoting Religion and where Religion is in contradiction with Science they would declare that Science is in a state of progress and tomorrow it may change its ground.

24. After the whole day of boring job of supervising same old softwares employed for monitoring the maintenance work of his universe in the 21st century how does God enjoys his time? Simple, by reading - *'Annalen der Physik.'*

25. Majority remains interested in knowing the truth. Few search for the truth.

26. Darwin wasted his important time and that of the scientific community in the most disgusting manner. He kept on luring the community in terms of facts and figures for arriving at the conclusion that humans have been derived from monkeys. I think, anyone could have arrived at this conclusion using immediate common sense.

27. Between Science and Religion lies God's brain.

28. Modern Theory of Evolution: social science people (except for lawyers) are creation of big-hearted God and the non social science people are creation of long-tailed monkeys. I am confused about the lawyers.

29. Science would always ask for more patience than Religion.

30. Majority of the world has been using Science as a product and it would have to pay for it.

31. The duty of human beings, other creatures, trees and nature in and after the 21st century is simple: to sacrifice their body in the progress of Science. Because after all it is all mortal.

7.1.3 Leadership, Politics, Governance, System......

01. Listen to all. This way you would waste your time.

02. Avoid explanations. This way you would compensate your time.

03. When certainty looks for validations and simultaneously validations looks for certainty, all what matters is leadership.

04. Making sure, that the energy of the coming generations won't get wasted in recovering from the problems extended by previous generations is a tough task.

05. The solution of corruption lies truly in the ignited minds of the school going kids for now and forever.

06. Competition cannot be controlled at the level at which it comes into existence. And along with certain benefits, it's most likely to march towards 'cheapishness' in various forms.

07. A politician should retire after ninety. And after the century, he should be legally issued in public interest.

08. A politician should go aggressive after crossing ninety. He should start telling people the truth, about the people.

09. Good politicians are most intelligent people, except they commit one mistake in their life.

10. Justice now, is just a matter of justification.

11. Politicians and people they always wait for each other for doing their work properly.

12. Changing procedure is more important than replacing objects. Something like don't try to control players just change the rules of the game.

13. Mother Nature taught us that those who have struggled have the right to exist. The identities need to be respected. However, the value of existence and identity should rise with each and every struggled moment.

14. Thinking in an evolutionary manner is more important than thinking in a revolutionary manner.

15. To bring qualitative changes in the education and systems, I think, is majorly a matter of joy for the politicians. And it's not going to be as simple as the 'Theory of Relativity' that deals in two simple subjects of physics and mathematics.

16. After ideologies, what is important for a leader is reading the outlook of the people and then making their 'read only' memory a 'read-write' one.

17. Now, we Indians don't require good politicians, we need a magician like Gandhi. 1% of him would be enough. Though we won't deserve even 1% of him.

18. Be your own leader, be your own follower, that's what independence is all about.

19. It would be good if children and young think of becoming heroes like Nehru and Radhakrishnan rather than Gandhi. If we could have those regular heroes in quite regular time, we would never need an irregular superhero like Gandhi.

20. A true leader is a person who can impress engineers of his or her nation.

21. Leadership in adverse situations is convincing people for doing right things in right manners and becoming the first to do so.

22. If you are impressed by someone try to make the person your subordinate.

23. Young should follow the greats then should get up to their shoulder with their support and should look far from them so as to fulfill their dreams.

24. Our domain of influence should always remain greater than our domain of authority.

25. The primary objective of the media is to provide platform for the politicians so that they can entertain people.
26. Media is not supposed to be just a mirror of the society. That's why it is not termed as 'mirror' I think. It should have three fundamental property of a 'media'. It should know what to absorb. It should know what to reflect and it should know what to emit. Though existing with

excellence under great competitive pressure is difficult, but this does not mean that things should remain dependent helplessly on pessimistic monopoly of news and should expect too much of the uncivilized control. A central and most rational voluntary regulation may work and is expected to be there.

27. There is only one way to go up against a system and that is its reformation. However, this would never mean that we should keep waiting for the reforms to be done. We should continue solving problems by applying best of our efforts.

28. The differences between a system and its successor or predecessor system are filled with chaos.

29. In a system emotions, feelings, sentiments, sacrifice should come at last.

30. Inspire people to be as self-disciplined as possible and design systems as less dependent on self-discipline as possible.

31. System should have measures to get out of its deadlock state.

32. Every system will have some overheads.

For generation of understanding related to a system, rule of thumbs would prove to be very handy, like:

- A reformed system lies somewhere in the existing system.
- A system would never be comprehensible in a systematic manner.
- System cannot be designed by considering any one to be a wise person.

- A system would always need some wise people.
- A system would always have some wise people.
- If a drunkard is saying that drinking alcohol is injurious to health, he is not wrong.
- Condition applies everywhere. Even on this statement.
- Fulfillments of objectives are more important than doing things systematically.
- If you have fulfilled your objectives without doing systematic activities then try to find out how that objective can be fulfilled by doing things systematically.
- Never fall in love with any system.
- Make your heart to think only if your brain is capable of circulating blood.
- A system is a set of all time small problems for you so as to safeguard you from big problems of sometimes.
- It's not about systems. It's about 'systematic-ness' and 'maintenance'.
- Never look for one or two examples in a system.

33. Now, directly or indirectly, knowingly or unknowingly, a politician would never be honest. Even if that were the case, then the smart people would say look he is pretending to be honest. So the last option for them would be that of being a schemer.

34. Now 'how' is more crucial than 'what'.

35. Corruption is the need of the hour. To an extent it is compensating for our systems weaknesses.

36. Success of a nation depends on how sincerely her old and young listen to each other and how rationally they understand each other.

37. We will have to find possibilities for stronger laws. At the same time we would have to find possibilities so that they would be used minimum.

38. Reservation: few of our ancestors tried to be over emotional in terms of knowledge sharing. We will have to pay for it.

39. I think first we need an Independent Regulatory Authority for Central Government (IRACG) and Independent Regulatory Authorities for State Governments (IRASGs). Something like Independent Regulatory Authority for Higher Education (IRAHE) is then supposed to be a part of the 'A' plan.

40. I think now we shall have to seek for some 'use and throw' laws as well. Few 'case dependent' laws also.

41. Can laws begin as being tough on crimes and end as being tough on ignorance?

42. Have faith on socialism. Have faith on capitalism. Be a follower of scientism. Persuade economists for putting tax on the use of integral calculus.

43. What can be most liked about the systems of politics and bureaucracy is the state of sincerity and dignity that they are supposed to maintain under all circumstances. But if something like House of Commons likes to enjoy the arguments of and of the order of vehement yet true Macaulay then few overriding should be welcomed.

44. Religion helps people getting rid of their fear. Who would come to rescue when Religion would fear?

45. Things are very simple now. What all anyone would have to do is the economic seduction of 7-8 politicians just and enjoyment and patience of a century or two.

46. Every discipline is build around certain goodness more than that exists normally in human nature.

47. Money makes it own path. We humans with regular business can define the path either as legal or illegal.

48. Education in the 21st century should help economy for caring for the society. Education in the 21st century should help society for compensating for the damages that the caring of economy would do.

49. When memories are becoming heavier on dreams a politician should plan of retirement. Why only politicians, everyone should do this.

50. I think, when young would become aware of the complex interlacing of authorities and responsibilities, the olds would simply make a way for them as their authority and as their responsibility.

51. I think the best way to move forward materialistically at state level would be looping of having 5-6 decades of capitalism then followed by around 2 decades of socialistic touch. And if this is not going to happen artificially its likely to happen naturally. Education could be the driving force and then should come the science of mental life.

52. For next fifty years plans should be there for having a controlled corruption rather than for controlling corruption.

53. True leader is a person who lives like a common man yet doesn't have the privilege of being a common man.

54. I don't think that God would be able to produce arguments against majority of the politicians for most of the cases. A first-year Law Graduate would be enough to hold him up.

55. Now in this civilized world a statesman would never be as honest as Mr. Niccolo Machiavelli.

56. We will need some men of principles; by hook or by crook.

57. Capitalism is an art of separating horses from mules and then utilizing them as donkeys for making more money. The more money is then utilized for providing opportunities and inspirations for mules so that they can work hard and become horse. All this has been promised for few centuries only.

58. Criminalization of politics: time and money of anyone in politics is a matter of democracy. To decide whether someone is a criminal or not is task of Laws. Who should take part in elections is headache of parties and constitution. Politicians are innocent.

59. Englishmen were experimenting with democracy and we have taken them seriously.

60. Reformations can be based on one word - 'justice' that is finding loopholes in laws.

61. God planned India's fortune in his summer vacations.

62. Majority remains interested in Macaulay's minute. Few remain interested in his hours, days, years, life and letters.

63. Fate of Democracy in 21st century would depend on how wisely she would accept the encroachments of Religion.

64. Nuclear weapons should be kept alive for impressing and entertainment of aliens and their kids.

65. People should always work with truth and honesty. Politicians should make sure that these people and families are not dying of hunger.

66. At times Laws is all about unnecessarily meddling between two parties in the name of being civilized.

7.1.4 Thinking, Greatness, Philosophy, Work......

01. Thinking, Greatness, Philosophy: ultimately, everyone needs some work to do.

02. The world is not an analogy. Analogies should be used to enrich understanding rather than for arriving at conclusions.

03. It is always easier to have and not to have faith on things. Both the cases won't take much of time and brain.

04. Certain jobs for their completion and success need more eccentricity than hard work and experience.

05. Professionalism: Work and let others work.

06. It's important that people should realize their mistakes themselves, but make it sure that it's not too late for them.

07. The world is too complex to generalize. Simply, it's a case.

08. I think the greatest sacrifice that we can perform for our nation is by doing our jobs sincerely.

09. Creativity and innovations are sort of 'anti-disciplinary' activities.

10. Professionalism in behavior when based on professionalism of work can only bring success to a team effort. Work should not be tried to be compensated by behavior.

11. Being professional and a normal person is like becoming someone who is suffering from split personality disorder.

12. Greatness may be an ephemeral concept. It is never concerned whether others know it or not.

13. However charming a philosophy of a thinker may be, it's good for society that he should not remain a useless fellow for long. Else, he would start convincing people to behave like him. That's why I think philosophy has been kindly declared as a separate discipline and governments provide stipend to philosophers also.

14. Thinking is a process that is expected to reduce the necessity of experience.

15. Never forget the paths after reaching the destination. Keep record of each and every step.

16. Our weapons are getting more and more civilized with passing ages.

17. Thinking is a process that is expected to enrich common sense contents of brain.

18. God is ought to be a confused mathematician.

19. Earth is God's HR testing zone.

20. Animals other than human beings are detectives of God.

21. Only aliens can bring unity on earth. Whether they will bring peace also with them that they will decide only.

22. It's almost impossible to know what lies there in the dark chambers of great minds until and unless they tell you the truth.

23. Complex thinking at different levels will simplify our world.

24. I think, it's not possible to have faith on a philosophy and at the same time to enjoy it by analyzing it brutally. Like, if you want to enjoy deliciousness of a food item you would have no option other than to take it in your mouth.

25. Optimistic thinking is based on two factors: Are desires there? And what a good person can do?

26. In this busy era, even thinkers should remain prepared for being asked for the guaranty of their thoughts.

27. Ultimate value of life lies in identifying and shouldering responsibilities properly.

28. In the end it seems that after years of hard work and thought processing, I have arrived at a conclusion, at which I could have arrived easily using common sense.

29. Fortune is a set of irrational reasons.

30. A genius might be a person who had already committed so many mistakes that he can easily pretend to be genius.

31. Experience whether good or bad is always useful and that's the beauty of experience.

32. Imagination is more important than knowledge. When u have got to the end of imaginations, it's good to have faith on things.

33. Understanding more with less of knowledge, leads to rational faith.

34. God favors braves and he remain confused what to do with philosophers.

35. God's greatest mistake is absence of ear lids. God's greatest creation is presence of two ears.

36. In this 21st century, an intelligent is a person who knows how a share market works.

37. Few philosophers are very effective but at times they become pied piper of Hamlin.

38. True intellectualisms lie in the joy of being unaccountable and yet praiseworthy.

39. The silence of great leaders is far more powerful then their words.

40. We, if interested, are obviously expected by the evolution to be more intelligent and complex than our ancestors. We always have more knowledge about our world, more history to analyze, more methodologies and approaches for solving problems than ever before.

41. Greatness may lie in taking revenge in most decent manner.

42. Intelligence always accepts the importance of experience, but experience rarely accepts the importance of intelligence.

43. Those who survive big blunders can easily pretend to be wise.

44. The superheroes of history would always remain there, but people will always look for the living legends.

45. There is something between confusion and clarity and that is abstraction.

46. Greatness lies in beautiful dreams, success lies in beautiful memories.

47. A person privileged with all the luxuries and comfort of living would either become a useless fellow or a genius.

48. Those who think well should think how they have come up to this position.

49. Greatness through wisdom is less likely to come systematically; it's likely to travel for long through chaos.

50. Genius are those whom words bring laughter with origination, become comprehensive after some twenty five years, followed after some fifty years and become common sense after a century or two.

51. Two philosophers can never be good friends. If a philosopher is found praising some else philosopher then that would mean time has come to take him to a psychiatrist.

52. It's very important to bring philosophy into executions through systems.

53. Your true role model would never leave you alone provided you are a true follower.

54. True wisdom lies in preventing your perceptions, developed after experiencing things, from turning into prejudices.

55. Intelligence derived from thinking is more important than that derived from experience.

56. The importance of experience mainly lies in managing things efficiently and dealing with insurgencies.

57. Necessity is the mother of invention. Eccentricity is the grandmother.

58. At personal level – 'honesty is the best policy'. At system level – 'policy could be a best honesty.'

59. True intelligence lies in determining where to utilize it and where not.

60. System Engineers are the smartest people on this earth. They would hire you as an Assistant System Engineer and would utilize you like a 'stereo-typist'.

61. Human requirement engineering would simply be a tool that would tell us what would be needed at any point of time: research, justification, decision or emotions. As a whole it would be just an alternative that would always seek for better solution from others.

62. Every civilization has its own ego due to which she diminishes her chances to learn from others.

63. There would be two kinds of optimistic thinkers: one who are really optimistic and other who pretends to be optimistic as the only alternative.

64. Time to start from conclusions.

65. Barrister turned Mahatma Gandhi was the luckiest leader of all time. I wish all of the present leaders could also have opponents so wise and so intelligent as he had.

66. Gandhi was a highly impractical man. And the most amazing thing about him was that he neither provided us

with any on paper solutions. That's where I think he was great and at the same time unsuccessful. Alas he could have focused more on maneuvering minds of his own kind rather than leaving behind the mindsets.

67. Gandhi: no one is forgetting him, no one is finding him. Those who are trying, as far as I can think, are not finding him as 'Gandhi', but as an alternative. So is the case with Religion.

68. In life it is not all about knowing what is right and what is wrong. At crucial times it is about choosing between less wrong and more wrong. And Macaulay was master of choosing the less.

69. As far as I can think, no one can love his nation and his world so emotionally and at the same time so rationally as Macaulay did with his efforts and ideas. In fact that order is not supposed to be needed now owning to the great efforts of many like him and at the same time I don't think we would ever be able to get it.

70. A simple formula for being great: do something so that people can curse you after some 100 years.

71. True sacrifice is supposed to be a completely and absolutely a personal venture.

72. An unprecedented, unparalleled, long mental hardship and a long mental hard work is due in God's to do list for the great and ancient Indian philosophy.

73. Humanity would never understand how helplessly the humanity for its unconscious large-scale implementation would depend on the self-interest of human beings.

74. Man comes as an animal. Woman tries to make them social. And finally man manages to become a social animal.

75. System and Mother are very much like each other. The importance and vitalness of both can be comprehended in their absence only. And both are rarely praised in presence.

76. Different disciplines are like different Religions. Majority is expected to know about one and to have faith on others. A few should know a bit about each and more about co-ordination.

77. Great men use to see dreams. Macaulay used to see only those dreams that are to be the realities.

78. Now that Englishmen have deservingly ruled the pieces of land of the homo sapiens, they can plan to rule the heart of human beings of the well-defined nations. The Sanskritmen and the Arabicmen could supply the required documents and literature wherever needed.

79. Interdisciplinary studies at times may get very strange solutions. Like when Saints like Karl Marx and Friedrich Engels invaded Economics the result was something like Socialism. Another example is like when Barrister Gandhi invaded Religion the result was India's Struggle for Freedom. Beware of interdisciplinary studies.

80. Majority remains interested in Adam Smith's practices of free trade. Few seem interested in his theory of moral sentiments.

81. After whole day of hectic work a common man would look for entertainment and not literature.

82. Our ancestors (Eastern + Western + Northern + Southern + Aliens) had already worked so hard that majority need not to apply too much of their brain and few would have to apply too much of their brain.

83. In this 21st century every discipline should think of self as in the service of common man. Even Religion.

84. Majority remains interested in Gandhi's eternal concepts of truth and non-violence. Few remain interested in his ephemeral concepts of hard work and patience.

85. Gandhi made God to scratch his head. Time to bother God again. Time for experiments with bitter truth.

86. One answer would solve majority of the truth searching queries - 'Do God uses 'show cause notices'?

87. Time for Englishmen to review their knowledge transfer skills. Time to be cautious while making money or social service whatsoever is the purpose.

88. In our comfortable zone we read about the struggle of uncomfortable zones of history. With every struggled moment in uncomfortable zones the size of struggle in comfort zone increases.

89. A democracy is a form of governance in which few wise people take the responsibility for caring for society and above all the responsibilities of being curious and imaginative and the later are also responsible for determining whether someone else is eligible for searching truth or not.

90. Two kinds of mistakes: listening sincerely to olds and not listening sincerely to olds.

91. Where there is a will there are a number of bills: rent bill, electricity bill, telephone bill, internet bill, ration bill etc. etc.

92. We can have a degree of Laws but we can never have a degree of justice.

93. Laws would prove to be a best friend and at the same time a bitter enemy. It would provide a way with lots of obstacle and in the end the destinations.

94. Machines have entered in 21st century now time for human beings.

7.1.5 India, People, Education......

001. Higher education for young is all about praising Macaulay and allies and the education people for its pros and the pros and analyzing self and around for its cons and the cons.

002. As a student I was much taken with Maulana Azad National Institute of Technology, Mahatma Gandhi Medical College, and Jawaharlal Nehru University etc. But I always remained curious about one thing why we don't have something like Isaac Newton Institute of Science or G. J. Mendel Medical College or Bertrand Russell University etc. also? We are to think globally now, as after 2135 we are to lead this world or more precisely the world is going to follow us.

003. Existence is deserved by those who know how important their efforts are for the coming generations.

004. Only those struggle who fight against injustice, rest they make their things go easier.

005. Our ancestors have paid a lot for earning freedom for us, a lot of families are paying regularly for its maintenance, and so we should at least utilize it properly, thankfully and rationally.

006. Industrialization of the education and considering humans as resources are two basic need of the hour. The problems

arising because of this need could be handled and solved easily in near future (about three-four decades).

007. To remove economic poverty we need more of mental richness. Not just generosity but justifying skills as well.

008. The role of a teacher is to teach less and inspire more.

009. Education in the 21st century and further, I think, would remain more a matter of impressing students and getting the job done rather than teaching them.

010. If you are loving your work and at the same time you are finishing it on time then I think you are supposed to be the happiest person on this earth.

011. Now in this age, mainly we need good humans who know how to make money.

012. We need an education system that can turn intelligence into wisdom.

013. The success of education given to students depends on the environment provided to them by their elders.

014. Our education always looks for master of ones, though needed in very small amount. Rest becomes master of none.

015. Homage to freedom fighters and great people of history is incomplete till their dreams are realized.

016. Books could be our best teachers and friends. We can take them where we wish. They taught us where we wish. They talk to us when we wish. They give us time to think as much as we wish. They never say a word, but say almost everything we wish to listen.

017. Reading is a greater art than writing.

018. Success of education system would now mainly depend on the approach to the knowledge.

019. The most fundamental solution with majority outlook could be the learning and acknowledging habits at different levels. We generally learn less from our history but acknowledge more, we learn more from rest of the world but acknowledge almost for nothing. Here learning would mean not just knowing correctly but following correctly as well.

020. Our nation remains highly impressed by her history. Her history is worth enough also. Her faith in their religious, cultural and traditional legacy is incredible. However, there is a problem from the beginning and that is giving a sense of superiority to spiritual knowledge over material knowledge at generic levels. This still reflects in the mindset of people. If we wish to become a super power nation the more we can found the way in our own history, the more in the history of nations those who have reached that standard.

021. Indian engineers are the most deadliest things to happen on earth.

022. Our nation with all its ancient wisdom and diverse cultures is a great nation but struggling with problems like poverty, illiteracy, unemployment presents an equally miserable picture. When she would get rid of these problems, she would become a nation of her own kind. Powerful yet soft hearted for all, a true leader.

023. One of the major drawbacks of classroom study is that it does not give learners the time for thinking, when it is

needed the most. A part of education should be freed from this classroom behavior. And after a time the classroom should become a discussion room for the scholars.

024. The curiosity of education should lie mainly in uniting people, irrespective of their caste, culture, Religion and especially 'discipline'.

025. There should be two main objectives of life: as a human being and as a human resource. The art of balancing between the two would give a beautiful meaning to life.

026. The primary aim of the education system is the proper and systematic adjustment of the synaptic weights, after then their efficient utilization is left for the learners.

027. Who says higher education lacks professional orientation. Since ever we have been using every discipline so professionally. The different discipline can be tried at three levels:
- Profession.
- System Logic.
- Social Awareness.

028. A very good teacher always remains with us and that is our life.

029. Educational reformations would need a very special discipline called 'Gandhi'. Details would be discussed later.

030. Nature and life are two best learning school.

031. Struggle: There are two kinds of fights: one against injustice and another against lack of conscience. Those who fight against injustice are great, those who fight against lack of conscience are not struggler but smart

people and those who together fight against injustice and lack of conscience are someone like Gandhi.

032. A child's curiosity is very important and charming until the queries are posed on you.

033. A big problem with curiosity is that it comes before intelligence. Again, a big problem with intelligence is that it comes before wisdom. Again, a big problem with wisdom is that it is likely to come after committing lot of mistakes.

034. We expect the education to become more practical and application oriented for the scholars, we should also think about the theory of sex.

035. Unfortunately, many scholars do not remain as serious for academics as they remain for the competitive or entrance exams.

036. In academics, you are supposed to prove yourself more intelligent than others. In competitions, you can get away by proving yourself to be less stupid than others.

037. Our nation right now is experiencing a very critical cultural age. Majority of young would switch-on 'FM', before switching-on their work. Majority of olds, somehow caring for their cultural heritage, seems upset by the increasing dominance of materialism and westernization. The solution lies somewhere in the two thousand years old India. The generation gap needs to be bridged. Few perceptions would never change and all should know them. The world, as young minds would sense it, would be quite different from the world, as the older ones would signify it. For old, it would be full of memories, achievements, experiences and meditations. For young, the sensations would be full of dreams, opportunities, raw-nesses and

celebrations. Nevertheless, work should be continued to be considered as worship independent of age and era.

038. A success of a nation depends on how her citizens work without supervision.

039. I think, we Indians can make the best out of least of the resources.

040. Education primarily, is a matter of learning and understanding, the significance and the scope of a curious and a thinking mind. The rest are the details.

041. The scholars should know how things have originated, developed and shaped through chaos, at least for small scale.

042. We should focus more on the thought generation process rather than just on their language of expression.

043. Knowledge: It is not about our capabilities but about our maturities.

044. In a nation like India, ruling with democratic principles, where success of systems is highly dependent on the citizens, teachers are the core for the social happiness and prosperity of the nation.

045. Macaulay was the first rational freedom fighter of India. Gandhi was second, till 1920. I think, he then give up to his solitariness. His mulishness may be his weariness, brought his hard work back to cipher as well as that of few of his western ancestors.

046. Any education theory now would be a byproduct of some beautiful reactants thoughts catalyzed by few absurd ones.

047. The first milestone towards reformation would not be convincing the people related to education but would be confusing them totally.

048. Our learning does not need anecdotes from lives of great people only but from the lives common men also.

049. Higher education reformations would need proper marketing, stuffs of entertainment and brand ambassadors.

050. Every thing important comes with a price, except the most important things like freedom, education system, laws of inheritance, theory of relativity, operating systems etc.

051. Education is for removing the stereotyped thinking generated by the education.

052. We have a very peculiar system of education. It cares and praises the students but it never understands them.

053. It is very important to separate what we are learning from education and that from the experience.

054. A sixty years old well-educated kid would be the most valuable resource for education reformations.

055. Our capabilities would never lie in creation of quality concepts but in getting rid of the superannuated concepts.

056. We can't and we shouldn't blame anyone for the problems of higher education. I don't think anyone can think of anything above academics. Also our academics needs to be strong enough that no one should be able enough to think of anything above academics.

057. We will need strong reasons for our education system other than that that our ancestors were following it.

058. We won't and we shouldn't expect anything from anyone until we are very strong at the design level. We need to make sure how ideas would fit into design and how design would fit into ideas.

059. Higher education reformations would start solving big problems at the rate of 0.7 % per annum after some fifty years.

060. True and talented lawyers would be the most crucial resource for any kind of reformation.

061. The best approach for curriculums could be having curriculums with approach.

062. Our education needs an ounce of spiritualism and tonnes of mundanity. At least till 2135.

063. We should always have strong reasons for our failures.

064. Getting rid of all English symbols (and not all values) in future won't be a big task. The process would take just few 5 - 6 decades and a mere sum of around $ 25 billion.

065. Education reformations would need more of fiction work than non-fiction.

066. Majority of education people need not to think about Politics. They need to think like a politician.

067. In our nation, every good opportunity for higher education should be converted into achievement. For this every opportunity needs to be grabbed with both hands.

068. The biggest problem with education system is that it is a system that creates a set of true disciples.

069. In a book, say on economics, the definition of economics should come somewhere in the middle of the book.

070. The best way to reform present system of education is by becoming a true disciple of the 'system'.

071. Logic behind the curriculum development. Why different subjects are together? Overview of the curriculum, why we are doing? What we are doing? What complexities and necessities led to the formation of the curriculums? What are the business processes around the discipline? All this can be considered for the young curriculums.

072. Had Macaulay and Gandhi were there in the same age, India would have been a superpower some twenty years ago. From exaggerated Macaulay we can learn 'what' needs to be done at system level. From over cooled Gandhi we can learn about the most difficult task the 'how' at personal level.

073. Common man is never wrong. Our education needs to learn a lot from his daily life and the circumstances in which he is shouldering his responsibilities.

074. Higher education reformations would not be only about setting right things, but also about setting things right.

075. One problem with our nation is that the easier we get the problems, the easier we get the peace of mind. Another problem is that the easier we get the problem, the easier we get the people to be blamed for those problems.

076. India doesn't need Mahatma Gandhi only; she needs to think about Barrister Gandhi also.

077. Majority would care for you and would be interested in providing wholehearted advices for you with the help of

their experience. Hardly would you find a person who would have time and brain for you.

078. We do not need education reformations so that people can follow it. But we need a reformation so that education can follow common people.

079. I think true examination of the education system would never lie in fighting against the ignorance of the ill educated, but in fighting against the premature western awareness of the well educated.

080. We need more flexibility in examination system: those interested in studies should study and those interested in helping the economy of the nation should do that.

081. Reading environment is a greater art than reading books.

082. The unification of the real time knowledge would not need a theory involving the history and memories only, but the future and dreams as well.

083. Supplying moral and ethical values to learners is more a concern of environment than books.

084. There is something special about Englishmen and that is they need not to see too much of beautiful dreams to change things. There is something special about us as well. We the Sanskritmen and the Arabicmen do not often believe in changing things but our dreams always remain beautiful.

085. Though we Indians are desperately looking for reformations, but truly speaking, we are not mentally prepared for any kind of reformation.

086. A true problem of education is one that cannot be solved by experience. Or simply experience cannot and should not compensate for the real problems of the education.

087. Few things about us are too perfect, to be common, like the language Sanskrit.

088. In an ideal world with broadband Internet connection, the present of a nation should be decided by the people who were getting paid for thinking some twenty-five years ago.

089. In today's education what need to be done by 10% is imposed and expected by 90% of the scholars and what needs to be done by 90% is being offered to 10% only.

090. I think our education system makes us too educated too understand each other or rather to confuse each other. The problem is not mainly with the education, it's more with the word 'system' attached with it.

091. You can get away with the omniscience of God but not with the curiosity of a kid, especially, if the kid holds a degree in Laws.

092. And finally the system of higher education may think of providing a free of cost compensation course for the people who think that the drawbacks of the present system of education have hindered their personal progress in anyway.

093. We people expect very peculiar things from our education. What, we should learn from common sense, we expect our education to teach us.

094. Your literacy plans would be viable if you can explain them successfully to an illiterate person.

095. People need to develop a democracy based on common sense.

096. The responsibilities of education in India are immense. It would have to teach people how to use roads, signals and dustbins etc.

097. I think what is impressive about ancient India is not her knowledge, but her justifying skills in poetic terminology and all those heavyweight and heavily misused generalizations.

098. For long higher education would be a matter of grabbing opportunities rather than expecting miraculous qualities from it.

099. Time has come that we should do our homework sincerely, and without taking help of anyone else.

100. An ounce of faith in 'disciplines' in the minds of majority would be more imp than tonnes of knowledge of 'systems' in few minds.

101. Though we may fail to provide world-class infrastructures to the scholars but we can provide world-class challenges to them.

102. We would need syllabus as sentimental as possible within the limits of formalities.

103. If after years of studies and planning if we are arriving at the same conclusions then this also should be considered and declared as a part of education reforms.

104. I think even software scholars first should learn to develop a small system solution without the help of softwares.

Before they learn the application of software engineer over information driven system they should learn how software engineering comes out of system.

105. Education should be now tried at people's level of abstraction.

106. Education now is not about great men and sacrifice. It should be about common men and taxes.

107. I think our education system has fallen in love with theories. Calculus could be a matter of love for Bhaskara and Newton but for rest it's simply a mathematical tool.

108. Regulations: I don't think our universities are going to get away so easily. They still would have to provide beautiful on paper solutions.

109. We need more present and more logic in our education rather than history and information.

110. Grass is always green in history.

111. History is a mystery for those who reads it, but don't live in it. It's important that history should be read as a drama rather than pages of information.

112. Time to respect natural forces and utilize the artificial ones.

113. The approach for education reforms would have no option other then to consider education and social science people as clients. Emotional clients. Except for lawyers.

114. I think now it is not about following principles but first finding and getting to the point from where the path of principles begins.

115. Time to politicize and bureaucratize higher education sincerely.

116. Time for higher education to plan to find sincere alternative of politics and bureaucracy.

117. Indian intelligentsia with their major ideas getting dust seems now tired and exhausted out of administrative complexity, unwillingness and conflicts. The last thing they can try simply is reverse engineering.

118. Research for few civilizations would first remain a matter of knowing enough to make a make/buy decision.

119. Higher education should also start as Kinder Garten: with pen and blank papers.

120. What do old parents deserve - isolation and old age home, or respect and care? I think the later set. Do we need any arguments in this favor, why we need to do like this? No. Now think about fundamental sciences.

121. After years of study and hard-work education people and knowledge intellect comes in the state of realization: either it's too late to be a politician or it's of no use of being a just another good politician.

122. Education is supposed to be a way of promotion of social awareness: when to take help of others, how to take help of others, when to help other and how to help other.

123. India and Indians are still too complex to be handled by exactly young. They should read a lot of good books before thinking about designations. And after reading a good lot of material you would find that the biggest complexity of we Indians is our simplicity. At times we are too simple to understand.

124. Majority does not remain interested in thinking like 17th century brains. Majority does not remain interested in knowing about 17th century sacrifices.

125. The biggest problem with the followers of democracy is that that we never got the time enough to understand the 'ABC' of systems but we are now fully aware of the 'XYZ' of them.

126. Gandhi was a storyteller who knew a bit about Ram and Rahim and who enjoyed and consumed a degree of laws from University of London and utilized it to an utterly unauthorized extent. Look how simple it is to write stories.

127. Gandhians are most smart philosophers on this earth. They still think that they can manage this world without their man. Gandhi worked for 24 X 7 for some 55 years so that we can consume him again as soon as possible. They, the Englishmen just used to left him alone. We, the Sanskritmen and the Arabicmen killed him and now we are looking for one more. That's a great idea.

128. Young people never underestimate the power of Gandhian Philosophy. It may seem odd from its package, but the inside has the power to make almost every odd even. A good leader can show the way towards strength, a supreme leader like him simultaneously for time being could compensate for the weakness of others with his strengths.

129. Gandhi's rich brain was actually made for the 22nd century. The present poor philosophers would take one more century to end the process of 'the search of the truth'. After that they would somehow plan for the process that he used to perform in the beginning of the 20th century - 'the experiments with truth'.

130. Gandhi's immense faith on the capabilities and intelligence of the western philosophers and administrators has proven deadly for us. So is the case with the politicians that followed.

131. I don't think there is much difference between Hinduism and Macaulayism. Both believe in a typical way in the 'law of emotional division of '*karma*'. The first depends on the Lords of heaven and the latter on the Angels of graves.

132. Cow gives us milk. West gives us Science. Neither we can imitate cow nor the West.

133. Now for time being we will need temporary and ephemeral concepts, as they are, of fundamental sciences rather than the eternal principles of honesty and truth.

134. Greatest sacrifice that common people can make in a democracy is by doing their work sincerely. And I wish that there work environment won't be there as an envy.

135. Do what makes you happy. Make sure that its not making other sad.

136. Now in this 21st century I think the scholars should know a bit about the social aspects of their discipline.

137. True joy would never lie in unification of knowledge but in its disunification after the unification.

138. After years of studies and hard work if you are arriving at the conclusion that education is something that is very important then this is something that is very important. Also majority of educational reforms would lead to just yet another etymological differentiation of words.

139. Majority has 'A' plans. Few keep 'B' plans.

140. It should be the joy of Education to make sure that Politicians are enjoying their work related to almost anything and it is should be the joy of Politicians to make sure that Education people are enjoying there work related to almost anything.

141. Our University Grants Commission (UGC) is the utmost industrious, utmost sensible and utmost patriotic organization of this universe. She has been working amazingly for 72 hrs a day: as a seasoned old, as an intelligent youth and as a curious kid. She is the only organization that has been inspiring the youth to shoulder their responsibilities properly and not to fight for their rights, in nation lacking money to utilize resources efficiently. I wish every nation could have Commission like our beloved UGC.

142. Since her infancy our UGC has been curious about one thing - why mom and dad of a 17-year-old student don't realize the importance of fundamental sciences? Only the politicians and the private sector together can enjoy answering this and related questionnaire.

143. UGC's pecuniary management policies can leave any middle class homemaker in blushes.

144. After decades of waiting for the discipline - 'Gandhi', UGC has planned to bring revolution with the help of 'interdisciplinary' courses. I don't know how many disciplines one would have to combine to match that one discipline. As far as I can think, for this, anyone would run out of the disciplines and in the end, while running behind the problems we will find a system - 'Macaulay.'

145. If your kids' institutes are under the control of the government then ask them that they need not to be curious and imaginative. That action should be declared as a punishable offense as well.

146. Dear parents, make sure that if your kids are curious and imaginative then they are doing so by following a research methodology (the beloved methodology of Central Governments). Else they would enjoy their work and you would have to pay for it.

147. The greatest problem with majority of young is that they think about money only. They should think about money and more money and more and more. In doing all this make sure that money is not making you and you are making money and money is not controlling you and you are controlling money.

148. Macaulayism and Hinduism both are unfortunate in the sense that they never got the opportunity to understand each other.

149. Macaulay never thought of us as others. We never thought of him as ours. We can afford common men hating him and intellectuals to pretend only.

150. The curiosity of higher education in the 21st century should lie in promotion of internationalism. And there lives a good delayed-nationalist in every immediate-internationalist by default.

151. Now the main focus of higher education should not be on marks but on moneys.

152. A big challenge for higher education would be how to combine 17th century thinking with 21st century actions.

153. As far as I can think there cannot be something like English curiosity, Sanskrit curiosity or Arabic curiosity or 17th century curiosity, 19th century curiosity or 21st century curiosity. It is simply curiosity.

154. We need something like People Sciences between Social Sciences and Democracy.

155. On the basis of my inexperience I can conclude that till 2135 India would and should remain in the hand of the experienced.

156. Macaulay thought that after going through the English system of education few of the people of Indian empire would have no option other than to become clever and lazy but unfortunately we all found ways to became sincere and industrious.

157. Gandhi thought that as now I have applied a lot of brain so my fellow countrymen and their descendants would manage with their hearts only. Alas he could have also gone through the readings of the sacrifice behind the development of integral calculus.

158. Few people have been planning for the court marriage of higher education with reality. 'System Ingeniouring - leave no discipline behind' would like the higher education to first fall in love with reality and then it would like to win the approval of the interdisciplinary guardians to plan for a social ceremony.

159. An educated person is supposed to be an education system for many.

160. Higher education is about knowing - for what it is higher and how higher it can be?

161. In a Democracy your job is likely to be done on time if you have an 'approach'. So approach is very important. Only higher education is lacking an approach.

162. An old person is a grown up child who is too shy to share his childishness with others.

163. We need education reforms, so that everyone can enjoy their boring jobs after some fifty years.

164. The biggest nuisance that has been created about the English system of education is that that it's an English system of education. I think it is something that is a natural fruit of curiosity and liberty. And now since we were behind in creating it naturally so at present we have no option other then to understand it in a language that is not so natural to us.

165. Cursing an education system that you have gone through without attempting for making it better is like making a hole in a utensil in which you eats your daily bread.

166. The task of education in the 21st century is to make common man's life as comfortable as possible because after all common man is no longer a common man. He has become 'a soldier of capitalism.'

167. Before creating our own system of education it would be mandatory for one and all that they should fall in love with present system of education we have.

168. Education in 21st century = 24 hrs of common man.

169. Education in 21st century = Life and Work.

170. Education in 21st century = When to take help of others and when to help others.

171. Ultimate Education in 21st century = To understand the limitations of Education - 'the system' and developing art to think above the limitations of the Education - 'the system'.

172. Education needs not to think about Economics but as Economics. If market is becoming heavier on education then this is just a beginning.

173. Few research institutions are based on contrary basis. On one side they believe in a classless society and on the other hand they have divided people in the name of disciplines especially social sciences, non-social sciences and lawyers.

174. Laws would expect the government to invest endlessly in laws. Education would expect the government to invest endlessly in education. Business would expect the government to invest endlessly in business and infrastructure. Domain 'XYZ' would expect the government to invest endlessly in the domain 'XYZ'. Government would think of making *'char'* more paisa by converting human beings into human resource. Saints and philosophers would declare the government as money minded.

175. Indian constitution needs dramatic amendments in the 21st century like consideration of wheat at Rs. 2 per kg and rice at around Rs. 4 per kg to non social sciences people whose ridiculous ideas may prove beneficial for the society of 22nd century.

176. Destinies of the Universe, especially of the Globe, now lies in the hands of UGC: whether she would have the mercy to Grant the leaders, the permission to traverse multiple disciplines to find more and more creativity, so as to bring reverse-evolution till 500 B.C. on the Globe.

177. Time to redefine educational background:
    Nursery to 10th - all major disciplines...
    11th to 12th - xyz disciplines...
    Graduation - narrowly defined discipline - X...
    Post Graduation - Further Narrowly defined discipline - X continued...

178. India neither needs young nor she needs old. What all she needs is *'bude bharat mein fir se nayi jawani.'*

179. As higher education is lacking money she could plan more intensively for downward filtration theories.

180. The biggest blunder that humanities and social sciences have committed is that that they have failed to include politicians in the list of bundle of desires.

181. Interdisciplinary courses would leave both the UGC and the disciples in a state of confusion. Disciples would remain confused whether to follow the main narrowly defined discipline or to come out of it time and again to bring creativity. UGC would remain in dilemma whether to pay grant to people sincerely following the discipline or to the people bringing creativity by moving out of their narrowly defined discipline. I think ultimately we will need some courses that would help us in getting rid of narrowness of human minds.

182. Everyone needs a bit of love and care: politicians, educationists and research scholars and above all lawyers and system engineers.

183. Time to see dreams with headers and footers.

184. Indian young are most insincere. They never plan anything so that their olds-can proceed for the *'haj yatra'* or the *'char dham yatra'* on time and without any tension.

185. Few people would care for you and would advise you to listen sincerely to your saints and Religion. Higher education would care for you in altogether different manner. She would not be satisfied until and unless she would bring a Saint out of you and that too of an unknown Religion.

186. Time for more councils, commissions and degrees like:
National Knowledge Backup Commission (NKBC):
Indian Council for Curiosity and Imaginations (ICCI).
Indian Council for Exception Handling and Overriding (ICEHO).
Bachelor of Justice.
Bachelor of Answerability.
Bachelor of loopholes in Laws.

187. Social sciences, humanities and education need not to worry about the philosophers of 12th, 13th,.......19th and 20th centuries. Their philosophies would be used for writing storybooks, and poems and for bringing daydreamers out of kids and young.

188. Our education system is looking for solutions out of part time curiosity and part time imaginations.

189. The biggest misconception of social sciences: God is a social scientist.

190. A good system of higher education is responsible for criminalization of politics.

191. Few commissions are too old and experienced to commit mistakes.

192. Economist's biggest misconception: research is something that needs patience and not intelligence.

193. Now since politicians claims to remain nearest to the reality so only they can enjoy bringing higher education to come to terms with reality.

194. Systems Ingeniouring would be an interdisciplinary approach meant for ending of the interdisciplinary habits.

195. A simple formula for raising the quality of education:

QAL(edu) = (TCH(sal) x QUT(con)) + ECA.

where

QAL(edu)	=	Quality in education.
TCH(sal)	=	Salary of teachers.
QUT(con)	=	Quantity of contents.
ECA	=	Extra Curricular Activities for teachers like cooking food, voluntary participation in elections, census etc.

196. Economists would be utterly disappointed with system engineers. They, the economists, are investing thousand of bugs in making a system engineer. And they, the system engineers, instead of thinking about the return of investment, have been planning for social service.

197. The present state of democracy is best for understanding the true meanings of democracy provided we remain interested in the reasons behind it rather then finding immediate wrongs and immediate rights in it.

198. Education reform can be considered as a duty of educationists but it is never going to be an opportunity of any one segment of society.

199. We have a very typical system of education it has been provided with lot of responsibilities but almost no authority.

200. Higher education is dying to engage with society except that of politics and bureaucracy even when it makes such a sincere society that never expected anything for itself out of higher education and research.

201. The best reform for higher education would be putting higher education at risk.

202. Who says Indian economy doesn't take risk for R & D? It has put the whole R & D at risk even the one that involves only pen and paper.

203. Before Reforms:

Higher education is a branch of social science that deals with the production of educational goods and management of the production process.

After reforms:

Higher education is branch of social science that deals with the production, distribution and consumption of educational goods and services and their management.

204. Higher education is more worried about job to every hand. Now it should plan more intensively for job to every brain.

205. Dreams, desires and education:

PhD (Education) for one and all.

106% of GDP in education.

A high-class research lab with every primary school.

A University within every 2 km.

Planning for 10 Nobel Prize per year.

Governments working at CMM Level 10.

206. Economy is worried about Foreign Direct Investments now time for economy to worry about some Foreign Direct Intelligence.

207. God's hit list:

Physicists:

Spreading rumor that physics is going to finish soon and hence underestimating God's intelligence.

Mathematicians:

Helping physicists in justifying their fictitious Science.

Economists:

Spreading rumor that research is something that needs patience and not intelligence. Believing in free trade but not in free thinking.

Lawyers:

For not leaving any loophole in laws. For not experimenting with laws.

Religionists:

For being clever and lazy.

Spreading rumor that God loves poem.

Philosophers:

Spreading rumor that God is weak in mathematics. Representing same thing in more than needed number of ways. For rumoring that west is end of the world and the world is flat.

Educationists:

Snatching bread and butter of curious and imaginative kids.

Considering education more important than food, shelter, cloth, employment and employability.

Declaring hard work of ancestors as narrowly defined.

Politicians:
For thinking about nothing other than politics and sacrifice.

Bothering too old people for consultancies.

For expecting nothing for themselves out of higher education and research.

Social Scientists:
For not including politicians in the list of bundle of desires. Spreading rumor that God don't love non-social science people and lawyers.

Social System Engineers:
poking their nose in others job.

Inspiring people for interdisciplinary studies without taking permission from beloved UGC.

208. UGC = Unfolding God's Cerebellum.

7.1.6 Problems, Solutions......

01. While (IGNORANCE >= KNOWLEDGE)

Loop

Print ("The problem is with me");

Scan (& Good_Books);

IGNORANCE = IGNORANCE -1;

KNOWLEDGE = KNOWLEDGE +1;

End loop;

Print ("The solution is with me");

Beware of the infinite loop.

02. Not every problem would have solution.

03. Biggest problem: When we have time for thinking about problems, either we do not have the problems, we do not remain interested, we may think it is not our concern to think over them, or we remain too small for them. And when we have problems and we are bound to solve them, we hardly get time to think about them.

04. No job worth in this world is easy, easier ones are made difficult by competitions. For still easier ones foolishness can do the job.

05. Solving problems and doing something for solving problems are two different activities.

06. Problems: Lack of persistence of curiosity and rushing towards conclusions.

07. At times, you would have only one problem and that would be: you have the on paper solution.

08. Problem cannot be solved at the level of understanding at which it is created. When finished with the levels, the only solution would be to find a new solution with 'inter-leveling' approaches.

09. Fewer supporter of extremism will not make much difference. The majority needs to think optimally.

10. Problem is not of principles but whether people are interested in them or not.

11. They would know future problems who would know solutions to present problems.

12. Don't believe in taking risk, but just know how to put easier and simpler task at risk.

13. Certain steps towards solutions would be highly strange.

14. Where there is a will there is a way. Where there is a complex will there is Systems Ingeniouring - leave no discipline behind.

15. Its always-easier not to remain in a state of confusion. 'Theory of Reasons, Profits and Loss' would help in decision making under the opposite situations.

16. Bringing a discipline out of 'indiscipline', a system out of 'disorderness' is very important for solving problems.

17. Problems become complex with time, but not human brain.

18. Staying longer with the problems is important. There would be a moment when there will be only three things: a pen, a paper and you.

19. Prejudices whether in favor or against are more likely to create problems.

20. Solutions are wanderers and are more likely to meet the wanderers. With time and efforts, the certainty of finding

its tips and tails within a particular area will increase, but the exact position will never become certain.

21. A problem can be mapped to a lack of fulfillment of a normal requirement.

22. The problem was with our ancestors. They failed to commit big blunders.

23. Don't generalize. Make your domain of consideration big.

24. Alone, a problem would be best defined.

25. Time has come when we should think of learning more from the problems and mistakes rather than the disciplines only. Problems have grown up more complex and smart than the simple and innocent disciplines and systems around us.

26. We need our education system to be as broadminded as the problems.

27. The biggest problem that our nation is facing now is thatthe work is not considered as worship as sincerely as it was before in books.

28. Problems do not have heart. They have brain only.

29. If you can't prevent the 'not so good' then give it a way.

30. Only two kinds of problems should exist: lack of money in pocket and lack of knowledge attached with dendrites.

31. Two major problems after fifty years would be lack of patience and lack of scientificness.

32. The greatest challenges against the humans civilizations after some fifty years would be the problems that would be everyone's problem, but no one's personal problem.

33. Few problems would never give us a chance to bounce back. Specially, the alternatives based on tactics and strategies instead of ethics and planning.

34. Global warming is not a big issue. The solution would hardly take some five to six months of 2050 and equipments of few hundreds of Rupees. Economists would solve this problem and would generate a lot of revenue and employment out of the problem solving process.

35. The roots of the problems are not just 60 years old but about 160 years old. May be only 320. May be only 640. May be only 1280. May be only 2560. Not more than this.

36. After around 2050 the term 'superpower' is going to be completely and absolutely meaningless. What would be more meaningful thereafter than the concepts of GDP would be something like GDH - Gross Domestic Happiness.

37. A superpower would be a nation who would be able to destroy the earth completely before losing the plot and can maintain this ability for twice in a century. I think majority of nations are worried about the maintenance ability.

38. For solving problems patience and direction would go hand in hand. Direction would come first.

39. So, so far we have successfully confined problems in the following list:

Absence of Broadband Internet.

Presence of laziness in bureaucrats of God.

Lack of money in dad's pocket.

Lack of Macaulay's writings.

Lack of desires.

Systems based on non System Ingeniouring principles.

Presence of misfortune.

Absence of misfortune.

40. Lack of scientificness is responsible for majority of the problems. Presence of scientificness won't be responsible for majority of the solutions.

41. Who the hell on this earth is finding problems with the systems based on non System Ingeniouring principles.

42. When conscience comes before curiosity.

When 'dharma' comes before 'artha.'

When technology comes before Science.

When information comes before knowledge.

When designation comes before desires.

When formalities come before objectives.

When management comes before planning.

When shyness comes before money matters.

When satisfaction comes before success.

When care comes before understanding.

All what is missing is reverse engineering.

'Students tend to progress from being concrete to abstract thinkers as they develop increasing expertise in a learning domain, and across the domains. This is to some extent a developmental process. However, it is also affected by other factors, such as levels of interest, context and the quality of instruction.

Concrete thinkers are likely to create meaning most effectively when knowledge and skills are developed sequentially, one step at a time, using logical processes. When students engage in concrete thinking, they tend to interpret information in terms of its practicality or usefulness. They have a preference for kinaesthetic or visual ways of receiving information, and tend to like questions that have an answer, rather than questions that are purely speculative.

Abstract thinkers are able to make connections and transfer knowledge with greaterflexibility than concrete thinkers. When students engage in abstract thinking, they tend to think in ideas or representations. They speculate about possibilities and conclusions, and develop beliefs on the basis of these. Abstract thinkers are more capable of building meaning in non-linear forms by creating patterns and overall frameworks. They are more likely to have insights in random ways.'- [Victorian Essential Learning Standards, Victorian Curriculum and Assessment Authority, State Government of Victoria, 2007].

Understanding at thought level of abstraction and elaboration of thoughts provides a good insight into the mental development process of the learning.

8

Rediscovering Learning

"The child is the father of the man"

-William Wordsworth

8.1 The Grounds Left Behind: The Unofficial Arrival at the Concept

Well it is all about the levels of abstractions and the levels of frustrations. Our ancestors like Aryabhatt, and Bhaskara-I were running alone and too much ahead of time (also British were too lazy in their campaigns). And there were never the chances to put great people like Bacon and Galileo behind the bars. I have arrived at the conclusion that majority of my Indian philosophers are not just the promoters of spiritualism but they are in deepest of agony -'why we don't have the credit of being the pioneers of physicalism as well?' Everyone wants to be no. 1, no one wants to be at 2 or 3. Everyone is willing to be powerful as soon as possible with as minimum efforts as possible, on the knowledge and efforts gained by others. No doubt we are going to rule this world and not the people and the body but their hearts and the soul and not for a century or two but forever but before becoming a world leader first it's important to learn for the kids and to learn by the kids. How?

Adam Smith has said people engaged in personal legal benefits sooner or later invisibly and positively affect the society. This is exactly the kind of engagement that should be searched for: the search for the legal universe outside and within.

When it comes to the legal universe in a democracy, holding people responsible for failures is very important. Who in general is responsible for the current scenario of system of education? Who in general would be responsible about the futurity of the system of education? The answers and the arguments would help in a lot of learning. My choices respectively are the God who designed Macaulay's brain and a doctrine that would confuse God with his designing skills. Still for mundane purpose:

Political system: As far as I can think, worst activities like the following also would have proven insufficient, for the different kind of on paper stabilities and feasibilities, without the real time applicability and application of complex systems approach both at the general as well as the special level of the different disciplines and systems and at the same time for reaching people's mind and heart with poems: few of our ancestors fallen in love with ignorant Macaulay along with our omniscient Gods or few of our ancestors fallen in love with the God of small beings along with Lord Macaulay. Yeh one important and the only thing always to be kept in mind would be their ultimate order of patience and sacrifice. So, say no to reincarnation, say no to revolution, and say yes to knowledge-based evolution. Democracy is a Religion in which God has faith on human beings. Our democracy is in its adolescence, need to take decision with patience and for long the decisions would bring just satisfaction, but at least. It is the right time to learn the ABCs of systems and get the people learned with the ABCs of democracy. A number of teachers are more concerned about why India is not producing Nobel Laureates (obviously because a number of politicians are bad) then the development of their kids. Now here is a chance for the system of politics to find out how these facts are connected to each other (would hardly take hard work of some twenty odd years). Lastly, do the system of politics is expected to follow the law of 'non-evolutionary division of mental labour'...? I am totally confused about it and would remain confused forever. Rest is Fine. One day is made of 24 hrs only.

Education system: In deep *'moha'* with Macaulay when she was supposed to be in love with him. If the 'too disciplined', 'too sincere', 'too obedient', 'too shy like a new bride' (all these attributes are basically a good sign for the far future of education), system of education (the political system is next in the list as the owner of these attributes all this basically is a good sign for the far future of 'millennium editions of democracy') could have asked and searched for the fundamental rights of even few of its fundamentally curious and imaginative kids...then...that would have been the wastage of few of our bugs. Rest is fine. And I don't think that anyone who has gone sincerely through present philosophy of education system would be hypocritical enough to think as cunningly as dirtily as the realities might be, but all this, for taming the problems.

So both the system should be considered as more far from any responsibility and ultimately system of engineering is potentially nearest responsible for the present situation of the system of education and system of engineering would depend on the tolerance, mercifulness and generosity of both the system as potentially nearest for finding the remedies and the vaccines as well, for at least this time. But here is a small problem - by the grace of few of our western ancestors the system of engineering is not eligible for thinking about the system of education because of lack of a relevant degree from the system of social science or education (the beloved disciplines of Central Governments) (I was thinking that the most important eligibility criteria for conjecturing about higher education reforms in our nation would be that of being a middle class '*baniya*'). Also I think the system of engineering would be less interested in the 'intelligent designs' of Saint Marx, Max Weber, Rousseau or Barrister Gandhi, Yeh that would always be interested in their silly dreams of making this earth a beautiful place to live in. Also for a bit long it would like to be called as system of engineering. So here is a great opportunity for this bit of problem to be solved mainly by the system of education and in the worst case by the system of justice. But need not to worry about anything. In the deepest, the widest and the most mysterious of the economic crisis, system of engineering won't be shy and hesitating of enjoying on the food, shelter, clothes, pen and paper derived from others pocket. Also, system of engineering would try its level best to put tax on the consumption of system engineering but I am sure that the efforts would fail in the hands of the creation of the big-hearted God and the lawyers and generations to come would have to pay heavily for it.

So lot of work to be done. Before that I think, it would be of the essence to mention here about the development of this approach. The intent is that it would be a very natural way of learning; the theoretical mechanization would be just a process for recreating more simple things especially for larger scale. Education and research in the 21st century would be less about teaching people but would be more about reaching them. For this multi-tier knowledge architectures would be needed.

The efforts and thinking at large were not dedicated towards finding out the concepts about the present education system or its problems, but simply the thought remain focused on the day to day learning process of students, the different disciplinary institutions influencing people and the problems and necessities of individuals, society, nation and civilizations. In short about the bundle of desires and the only twenty-four hours they have in a day.

This engineering approach has a limitation: it is not capable of moving ahead in continuation of existing concepts. It starts from the very basic requirements and considers, collects, reuse and reforms the elements (both tangible and intangible ones) that come in the way in moving towards the requirement fulfilling processes. There is nothing to be forced. Also things should go minimum in terms of patches. And I think in moving from one system to another reformed one, a centralized coordination of concepts, analysis and design would be very beneficial. Here a simple rule of thumb would be useful- "Masters of one would always need some jacks of all". At the same time this one is always there - "A nut of '10' number would need a spanner of the same number, '10' spanners of '1' kept together won't work".

An unofficial remembering of how this concept came up. Few broader points:

- Academic knowledge about life science, physics, chemistry and mathematics.
- Personal religious studies of Jainism and readings of literature, scientific philosophies and history.
- Academic knowledge of computer science subjects, systems engineering and object modeling language.

- A superficial knowledge of economy and necessities of our nation.

- A general awareness about happenings around and how they are related to present state of social systems.

- A need and search for a platform for system reformations.

- Covering of systems, their comprehensive understanding, studies and reformation possibilities, project management, implementations and system maintenance activities with systems engineering approach.

- Classification of knowledge under different headings.

- Finally classification of knowledge with two super-classes with each class having two subclasses as:

- **The knowledge of disciplines:**

- The knowledge of laws and principles.

- The knowledge of capabilities and maturities.

- **The knowledge of systems:**

- The knowledge of existing systems.

- The knowledge for engineering systems.

A cocktail of social systems and computational science based on the knowledge of natural science and awareness of its history. Simple. Anything left, yes, lots of stupidity and lots of mistakes (Don't worry no more 1000 pages). No curriculums are made for creating brains of this kind or that, but for making sure that mistakes and the backtracking committed by one generation need not to be repeated (the similar ones only) successively by successive generations. There aim is to take knowledge further for the welfare and comfort of generations to come as soon as possible. Interesting.

8.2 The Road Ahead: The Future Prospects and the Waiting Efforts

Human engineering would simply be a classification of knowledge to identify, assemble, arrange, present and apply it systematically for fulfillment of necessities by promoting understanding and thinking. The concept may prove to be satisfactory in social domain of work like higher education, system reformations, policy-making and procedural-designs, and of course for science fiction writers as well. For this first it would need to be developed as proper school of paid social service.

The thought would be primarily oriented towards socio-needs. The core concept would be as described by the models. The work to begin with would need a number of 'chaos-philes' for discussion and documentation over the issues of higher education highlighted in the gone chapters and a comprehensive approach for preparing artistic story books for different macroscopic discipline, systems engineering and knowledge engineering for young minds. Next refinement should be no less than writing and collecting about 50 books with developmental academic touch and the second next refinement would be a collection of some 5000 books. So a total of just 5050 books and that's something certainly I am not planning to do alone. So, if wishes are there for our nation to be a knowledge based society some 'Mr. Know All' would have to be knowledge warehouse, knowledge bullies, knowledge umbrella, knowledge cap, thinking machines, knowledge merchant, mobile library etc., so that it can be determined how much knowledge should be there in different brains and at what level of abstraction. Majority should be dealt at poetic level of abstractions as for them society, relationships and life would neither be a matter of systematic study nor it would be a subject matter for applying engineering tools. And this all could be done in the joyability of science and as the joyability of science. Patience would be the ultimate key for success. It's not like that apple fall on Newton's head in one afternoon and he wrote down calculus on the same evening. It took him 2-3 years in rewriting his pages of hard work that were burnt out accidentally. It took Kepler 17 years for arranging five symbols as $T^2 \alpha a^3$. It took Darwin a long time to determine that human beings are byproduct of a long chain of monkey's love making. It took Gandhi about 55 years to finally unite people. It's not like that on one day he was out of the train and on the platform he became the follower of truth and non-violence. He took time and patience for making his brain and his heart to work in synchroneity. And that too was a shortcut. Anyone else would have taken 500 years. It took us long to understands photon's relative eccentricities (in fact the truth is that that we have no other option). It took clouds a lakh year for making the magnificent oceans and it took nature millions of year in the creation of man and what modernity our Western ancestors achieved after centuries of mental sufferings we got in a 'minute'.

8.2.1 Disciplines:

The presentation could follow an evolutionary approach as the discipline has been developed over ages in terms of its origin, importance, development, merits and demerits. Some of the broader issues that would need covering, say in 'political science discipline', would be:

- History of political science, as the concepts has evolved in centuries and has taken shape today.
- Various political orientations.
- The current ideologies of political science.

- Political system presently in function.
- The laws regarding political systems and governance.
- The political psychology, political behavior, political logic and political statistics.
- The political problems. The solutions or the measures under consideration.
- Implementation difficulties.

Again every discipline would have its own issues and challenges.

8.2.2 System Engineering:

As discussed earlier, systems engineering would lead to the understanding of the systems, analytical and holistic approach for understanding the problems and various system elements and needs, proper documentations, presentation of problems, finding alternatives, designing solutions, testing of reformed concepts and managing activities. The document regarding systems engineering would need a comprehensive analysis before presenting it in a proper and systematic manner from social point of view. Some of the issues and guidelines that would need consideration would be:

- History of systems approach and its evolution.
- Study of systems sciences as it is in various social domains.
- The knowledge of the existing systems and systems presently in function.
- Revival of systems engineering research from social systems development. We will have to personalize it from our point of necessities.

- Application of approach on two-three macroscopic domain for finding elements, patterns and behaviors so as to bring the theory in a more disciplined manner.

- Finding possibilities of a generic theory. Though we would never fall in love with this approach and too much of generalizations would not be needed.

- A document to be written in academic fashion with simple case studies.

As discussed, never fall in love with system engineering. Use it and then don't throw it. Keep it alive so that tribute can be paid to it. Systems and disciplines are not conflicting to each other but are supposed to be complementing each other. Systems can always run in background and people would be expected to fall in love with the disciplines and disciplinary peoples only.

8.2.3 Knowledge Engineering:

Learning is simply acquiring knowledge and education is simply a formal support for the process of acquiring knowledge. So, knowledge is the core of the concept. Rest is.for redesigning, developing and maintaining knowledge-based system. The significance of knowledge engineering would lie in handling the comprehensiveness of the required knowledge base through its systematic presentation and in maintaining its comprehensibility. The majority should deal with the knowledge concept in terms of a single discipline, social awareness and need orientation related to that discipline. Issues and guidelines would be:

- A knowing about knowledge engineering approach, knowledge management and their fundamental concepts.

- Issues of knowledge identification and collection, separation, classification, representation, behaviors. The purpose and significance of knowledge.

- A study of application of knowledge engineering techniques in solving social problems.
- Finding new possibilities for knowledge representation for academic contents and knowledge regarding social domains.
- Development of knowledge structures and models.
- Thinking and presentation with inductive and deductive reasoning.

As in this busy world no one would get time enough to go through the hundreds of pages of reports generated so an important aspect of this approach would be the presentation of knowledge and texts so that their intents can be well understood with investment of minimum amount of time and brain.

8.3 **Rediscovering Learning:** Moving from 'Chaosphiles' to the Sensible Learners

In the efforts and approach for moving towards reformation of education system, the major short-term, long-term and super-long term guidelines, issues, reformations that would need consideration would be:

8.3.1 Issues Regarding the Present Approach of Learning:

Addition of new thinking dimensions to the comprehensive study of problems of present education scenario: from concepts to implementation problems is the need of the hour. Implementations accompanied by major changes would only serve our objectives. After higher education, brains should obviously move on for the entire system of education. Presently, for the sake of completeness highlighted here are few of the major guidelines calling for reorganization concerning the reformation of present education system and again some unsmooth points:

- **Rethinking and Reusability:**
- Too general to say: assembling of knowledge of existing works, researches and efforts going on and their maximum reuse.

- A large-scale collection of views, reviews, suggestions of students, teachers, parents and guardian, trainees, facilitators, human resource specialists, educationists, academicians, experienced domain specialists and research scholars.

Don't reinvent the wheel. Learn a bit about its origin and evolution and then focus on the latest design and the latest needs. Also never look at the wheel with any kind of suspicion.

- **The Ancient Touch:**
- Study over the various educational approach that prevailed in India since ancient times. Imbibing of the inherent valuable ideas and finding possibilities how they can be absorbed in our system of education with contemporary culture, traditions and examples.

And this would not be for impressing anyone but would help in fulfilling the self - concerns of promotion of the art of living and the art of money making through education. It doesn't matter where anyone would land - to hell or to heaven but all that should happen after going through a quality education. And it's not like that the age of Religion is over but it is yet to come. The only problem was that that someone didn't changed syllabus for 3000 years, so someone would need to have patience at least till 2135. Need not to worry about anything after the whole day of hoo-ha and activities, that they always deserve, kids, with the dark, are likely to come back in the mom's arms. God would open his last cards when man would think he has won the gamble. Remember God is far smarter than human beings.

Also any skeptical approach for concluding that the religious studies and more of character orientation may prove anti-economic need to be reconsidered, instead that would help in more and more economic growth in an all-together different manner.

- A collection of statements of various Religious books.

This would help in winning cases with minimum amount of arguments, time and effort. Also I think Religion and only Religion can provide a way for dealing with people when 'knowledge distance' becomes a heavy problem. Keep all this 'a secret'.

- **The Gifts and the Propensities:**
- Program for identification of gifted talents and natural inclinations.

- Issues of counseling and guidance at different levels especially for students at remote areas.

- Issues of career objectives according to interest, capabilities and maturities of the scholars, requirements, availabilities, better alternatives.

- Possibilities and consideration of parental counseling wherever needed.

- A study over gifted people and research oriented thinkers.

- **Language and the Mathematics:**
- Expressions should be kept at the top priority.

- Redesigning syllabus of Mathematics with greater orientation towards physical meaning of mathematical concepts, application oriented problems and generalized problems.

- Rethinking about the approach for Mathematical learning.

Use of calculator should be encouraged from kinder Garten.

- **Cramming, Rot Learning and Learning:**
- A study over cramming and rot learning. Finding their reasons, benefits, losses and alternatives.

- Orientation of evaluation system in accordance to the alternative approaches.

- Rationale and feasible flexibility in the system for special cases of examination results.

- Further possibilities for team work orientation, problem solving, and system orientations. Possibilities for every subject to be 'interdiscipinaried' with the moral and ethical presentation should be searched. Life with concepts:
  - Newton and Development of Calculus.
  - Lord Krishna and Mahabharat War.
  - Gandhi and Freedom Struggle.
  - Darwin and Theory of Evolution.

  etc.

- A study over the institutional obligations of the concerned human resource.

- A study over the various needs of the students: from concepts to academic performances.

At higher secondary level we can plan for something like a bit of information engineering. This would develop designing skills and understanding accountability of system in terms of relevant information.

- **Competitions, Coaching, Stress:**
- A study on the stress arousing issues as it is increasing on school going scholars. A rethinking about the contents and its feasibility from neurobiological perspectives.
- An extensive revision of the contents. Evolutionary pattern of learning and teaching with example oriented approach.
- Possibilities of parental learning in typical cases.
- A review on the frequency of the tests and examinations and other concerned issues.
- Issues regarding the competitions and coaching institutes. Revival of rules and regulations for them.

States could focus more on teaching methodology. Make sure that the premature provisions of opportunities are not bringing damages. Don't get trapped in the calculations of others. Together state and coaching institutes can plan for some sort of social service but only for deserving candidates. State could do this separately as well.

- **The Higher Contents:**
- A fresh developmental orientation of the theoretical contents.
- Evolutionary understanding of fundamental concepts.

Give the scholars a blank paper and a filled pen and the world of problems and ask them to provide generalizations and solutions. Simply, let them design bit of things first.

- Raising the degrees of mathematical, application and practical orientation for technical education.

- Long-term projects with real time approach.
- Scheme of different weightage to different subject or
- Distributing specific subjects among different groups of the same class would save a lot of time. This point can prove to be very beneficial from point of view of research as well as applications.
- Learning coordinators more focus on individual scholars: all time head ache for the scholars.
- Possibilities of real time projects.
- **The Faculty:**
- A consideration on the roles and workload of the faculties in higher education.
- Finding possibilities with dedicated faculties or dedicated time for:
    - Mathematical, practical and application oriented problems.
    - Personal learning and development programs.
    - Project developments and case studies.
    - Preparation for industrial training programs.
- Initial teaching documents and teaching manuals to partially get rid of the approach that is there in the academic books.
- **Research Orientation:**
- Thinking for syllabus dedicated for research scholars.

As said earlier experimenting with a much stronger research and development framework would only give enough flexibility to design and experiment curriculum-framework with dedicated professional and vocational-orientations.

- **Professional Orientation:**
- Further orientation of professional courses from the needs of relevant industries. Factors for improvement of efficiency of learning.

Like budding civil engineers can be punished to listen to two civil engineers discussing rather disputing over things at a construction site and then the buds can be asked to prepare a technical document out of their hot discussion.

Also since majority of the companies, say the software ones, have no other option, in this competitive world, other than to use reverse software engineering paradigms to work for, so too much of idealistic approach of study should be avoided till......

Also no education at present or later can supply the exact need of the market. The industries could be expected and supported wherever required to include Religious sermons and Spiritual lessons in their training programs. More proper work place, real time documentations of various industrial and business processes also needs to be there (the education can introduce the developmental importance of documents for understanding, sharing knowledge, avoiding conflict stimulating situations and the habits of reading and writing). For all this 0.000000000001% of relaxation in taxes for the relevant industries can be considered.

Expecting that a good commerce graduate would do accounting immediately and perfectly after emerging from the system won't be considered as a good one. Yeh he or she would be expected to know how to build up the logic in the real time environment with certain amount of experience. That's what education might focus upon. Concepts should build around planning.

Three-four months and eight subjects to be covered by a management student: such situation needs to be reconsidered.

A managerial development approach can be searched for its feasibility.

If someone belongs to MANIT then, he or she may know a little about the Maulana Azad: like he who never attended any school or college and finally became the first education minister of his nation. Now this would be something like a nonprofessional orientation.

If students of Barkatullah University are complaining about a weakness in a certain language then they should know that Maulana Barkatullah mastered seven languages and all by his efforts. Now this again would be something like a nonprofessional orientation.

Scholars, there is no alternative of education likewise there is no alternative of experiences. So keep proper documents of them specially that of the bad ones.

Further all possible formal and conventional extent of making higher education as sentimental as possible should be made.

- Revitalization of personal development programs at various institutes.
- Inclusion of 'Relevant Work and Professional Ethics' course.
- Something like 'The Indian Philosophy of Work' can be developed with present environment.
- Inclusion of subject like Business Process Development coupled with small projects related to subject domain wherever feasible.
- Rethinking about industrial training or end term training program.

- A study over various training programs at business organizational levels, the technical, application and human resource need of the organization for bridging the gap between the courses and profession requirement.

- Every sustainable possibility of private sector interventions for finance and intellects.

- **The Governance:**
- A thinking on the policy and controlling aspects for the institutes of higher education, administrative interventions, their autonomous behaviors and rights and responsibilities of the faculties.

As far as administration is concerned pre-college education would ask for a central control for consideration. This would help in deciding which features of study would need centralization and which decentralization. The post school education would seek for a gradual shift towards maximum independence and minimum regulations. People interested in independent regulations should be provided with more time, money, resources and an advanced *'sarkari'* methodology so that they can decide more precisely what they wish to make out of higher education. Also government should plan so that higher education can be made a headache of an independent authority as soon as possible. Experiments on smaller scale should be planned.

8.3.2 Issues Regarding The Human Engineering Approach of Learning:

The human engineering approach would take a long way through research, planning and development, before it could be presented as a proper school of thought. Still, together with a proper preparation of the contents, the following major issues and guidelines would need considerations from the very beginning:

- **The Knowledge and Evaluation:**
- Academic preparation of knowledge base of various domains.
- A syllabus for systems engineering domain.
- The design of evaluation and examination system.

- **The Validation:**
- The testing approach of the programmes with part-to-whole approach.

- Continuous monitoring of the system from various perspectives.

- **The Learning Programmes:**
- For the social systems engineers and the domain specific consultants within the domain of education.

- For some fresh young dynamic thinking minds.

- For the teachers and for all the facilitator's hierarchies.

- **The Integration:**
- Issues of integration with existing programs.

- Reconstituting of the very fundamental structure of the education system as required.

- **The Intellectual Distance:**
- A lucid preparation of the concept to minimize the intellectual gap that should arise in case of acceptance of reformed system of education.

Ample amount of research is going on or has been done in almost every domain from different aspects related to the learning process and education. A lot can be learnt from the education models that other nations are following for themselves and from the people working on them. For this approach it would be beneficial to centralize knowledge relevant to education concepts and system by dealing it at different levels of abstraction. An efficient way would be the interaction of comprehensive amount of human resource from different domains, and further analysis and discussion. This would generate a lot of new ideas along with the existing ones. And the most efficient option would be to have after intense planning a separate study group may be an Institute that would study in detail the research and plans of various institutes and would prepare an abstract of system of higher education from various aspects with the human engineering approach.

8.4 The Convergence:

Human engineering learning philosophy would believe in solving problems in normal, optimal and evolutionary fashion by learning from creations of nature and creations of humans. It would have its faith laid upon a number of disciplines that have already touched the horizons of philosophical perfection for serving mankind and humanity and would count on them. Whether it will prove to be perfect for us would be a matter of further research, development, planning and strategies for about next two - three decades. Truly, it will not search the better systems, but would try to encourage human potentialities to compensate for the limitations of the systems. It will not search for the solutions or the problem-solving abilities but the desires for the freedom and the dreams beautiful.

References

[RSP01] Pressman, R.S., "*Software Engineering a Practitioners Approach*", McGraw-Hill Higher Education, 5th Edition, 2001, pp. 245-47, 256, 299, 335.

[INC02] "*INCOSE Second Edition Handbook*", INCOSE TP 2003-016-02 Version 2a, p. 12.

[THO03] Thomé, Bernhard (1993). *"Systems Engineering: Principles and Practice of Computer-based Systems Engineering"*. Chichester: John Wiley & Sons.

[DES04] Bhatnagar, Suresh, Anamika Saxena and Sanjay Kumar, *"Development of Educational System in India"*. Vinay Rakheja - C/o R. Lall Book Depot, Meerut, pp. 198, 199, 287.

Further Readings:

The understanding behind the general idea has been absorbed by regular academic studies, general awareness books, news, articles and magazines. Some notes and books are referred in the text itself. Some other influencing books are:

01. Bhatnagar, Suresh, Anamika Saxena and Sanjay Kumar, *"Development of Educational Systems in India"*. Vinay Rakheja - C/o R. Lall Book Depot, Meerut.
02. Narang A.S., *"Democracy in India - Issues and Challenges"*, National Council of Educational Research and Training, 2003.
03. Thakur, Ghashyam, *"Challenges and Problems of Reforming Higher Education in India"*, Sanjay Prakashan.
04. Celly Ashok, "Towards a New Paradigm in Higher Esducation", Kalpaz Publications.

Index

W

Y